Series / Number 03-034

Clients Evaluate Authority:
The View from the
Other Side

CHARLES R. WISE
Indiana University

 SAGE PUBLICATIONS / Beverly Hills / London

Copyright © 1976 by Sage Publications, Inc.

Printed in the United States of America

For information address:

SAGE PUBLICATIONS, INC.
275 South Beverly Drive
Beverly Hills, California 90212

SAGE PUBLICATIONS LTD
St George's House / 44 Hatton Garden
London EC1N 8ER

International Standard Book Number 0-8039-0628-5

Library of Congress Catalog Card No. 76-21141

FIRST PRINTING

When citing a professional paper, please use the proper form. Remember to cite the correct Sage Professional Paper series title and include the paper number. One of the two following formats can be adapted (depending on the style manual used):

(1) OSTROM, E. et al. (1973) "Community Organization and the Provision of Police Services." Sage Professional Papers in Administrative and Policy Studies, 1, 03-001. Beverly Hills and London: Sage Pubns.

OR

(2) Ostrom, Elinor, et al. 1973. *Community Organization and the Provision of Police Services.* Sage Professional Papers in Administrative and Policy Studies, vol. 1, series no. 03-001. Beverly Hills and London: Sage Publications.

CONTENTS

Clients Evaluate Authority: The View from the Other Side

CHARLES R. WISE
Indiana University

1. INTRODUCTION

From Weber to the present the question of authority in organizations has been a much studied and discussed concern in management. In public management, theory and research have concentrated on the significant additional variables introduced into superior-subordinate relationships because of the public nature of the enterprise. The relationships between elected officials, appointed executives, career managers, and other public servants have been the appropriate subject of a substantial amount of research and discussion.

In recent times, however, another set of concerns has called for significant attention—those that deal with the interactions of public servants and public agency policymakers with clients and citizens. Citizen participation in program and administrative policymaking is now a central concern in public management. For the most part discussions in this area (Cunningham, 1972; Strange, 1972; Yates, 1973) have been concerned with the adequacy of mechanisms to provide for citizen participation in the organization and its management. The problems incurred in attempts at increasing citizen participation are receiving considerable attention (Herbert, 1972).

These studies have raised significant questions with respect to how clients and citizens generally perceive the role of those who administer the service organizations with which they are concerned, as well as the role of the larger governmental system of which the organization is a part. One of the questions is the degree of client-perceived legitimacy attributed to authorities who not only govern the services on which they depend, but who also impinge on their lives in other ways. In short, those who direct administrative service agencies as well as political authorities at several levels of government seem to have had their legitimacy to govern questioned from serveral quarters at an increasing rate. The events in Vietnam, the Great Society Program, the campus uprisings, and Watergate seem to have exacerbated this condition.

However, while there has been considerable research into such topics broadly expressed as political trust and alienation, little has been done to chart the nature of the orientations of particular client groups toward the authorities who govern their service organizations and the political system of which it is a part, and to determine the significance of those orientations for participation in the organization. A problem endemic to organization research is information on clients, although significant research findings are now beginning to be presented (Katz and Danet, 1973). According to Blau and Scott (1962: 74):

> One serious shortcoming of most organizational research, including our own, is that there is no investigation of the publics related to the organization. Studies of organizations have not included within the scope of their analysis the publics directly in contact with the organization, let alone the larger public which is potentially in contact. The neglect of this aspect of organizational research means that a one-sided picture of the official-client relation has been constructed: we are beginning to know something about the orientations of officials to clients, whereas we know little of the orientations of clients to officials and organizations.

One public organization in which executives have experienced considerable challenge in terms of the legitimacy of their authority is the university. During the period from 1967 to 1970 the level of protest activity was noticeably high, and at several points this "protest movement" seemed to constitute a major threat to the continued operation of the American system of higher education and possibly even to the operation of the political system itself. In short, organizational authorities appeared to have lost legitimacy among clients to the point that they were unable to govern the functioning of the organization or possibly even ensure its survival.

It is possible that this condition did not emanate exclusively from student concern over specific educational policies or decisions made by university authorities. The difficulties experienced by university decision-makers seemed intimately connected to events in the wider political system and to decisions made by other system authorities.

Several interesting questions arise. In terms of client orientation, are organization authorities evaluated in terms of legitimacy along with other authorities in the political system or are they evaluated differently? In times of stress do all authorities lose legitimacy equally among clients or do clients attribute legitimacy differentially? What are the antecedents of legitimacy orientations? How do clients feel about the regime of the political system? Do legitimacy orientations affect a client's disposition to engage in political activity or are ideological predispositions that are triggered by particular events more controlling? These are some of the questions explored in this paper.

AUTHORITY AS A CONCEPT

Authority within organizations and in government has long been discussed by political and organizational theorists and definitions are plentiful. It is difficult to extract similarities from any series of definitions, but it seems that most emphasize one of three attributes:

(1) the right to issue commands or orders by those exercising it;
(2) the general acceptance of commands by those subject to the commands;
(3) the relationship of interaction between those who command and those who obey commands.

Definitions of the first category focus on the position, office, or the source from which a command is issued, or the institutionalized nature of the control exercised. For example, MacIver (1947: 83) defines authority as the "established right to determine policies and act as leader." Parsons (1958: 210) describes it as "the institutionalization of the rights of 'leadership' to expect support from the members of a collectivity." The definitions in this first category assume the commands or exercise of authority will be followed by those to whom they are directed. The question of acceptance is assumed.

The second category of definitions focuses on the acceptance of the authority commands or relationship, or on the voluntary nature of the compliance with commands, requirements, or orders. Acceptance here is not assumed but must be gained. Bernard (1968: 163) states:

Authority is the character of a communication (order) in a formal organization by virtue of which accepted by a contributor to a 'member' of the organization as governing the action he contributes; that is, as governing or determining what he does or is not to do so far as the organization is concerned.

De Jouvenel (1957: 29) refers to authority as the faculty of including voluntary assent. Authority is excercised only over those who voluntarily accept it. Discussions of authority focusing on its acceptance often define it in terms of "legitimate power." As an example, Dahl (1963) refers to authority as "legitimate influence." The idea is here that if an official action is not accepted or perceived by the individual as legitimate, it is not authoritative but connotes something else, possibly coercion. The emphasis in these definitions is on the acceptance by those subject to authority and the considerations affecting this acceptance.

The third group of definitions stresses the relational aspect of authority. These are concerned with the relationship between those exercising authority and those subject to it. Friedrich (1963: 226) defines authority as "the capacity for reasoned elaboration . . . in terms of the opinions, values, beliefs, interests, and needs of the community within which the authority operates." Presthus (1960: 87) stresses the transactional view:

> Authority, too, is not a static, immutable quality that some people have while others do not. Rather it is a subtle interrelationship whose consequences are defined by everyone concerned. The process is reciprocal because each actor tries to anticipate the reaction of all participants before he acts.

Definitions of this category focus on the process of interaction rather than on the actions of either those in command or those who receive commands.

While it is definitely useful to adopt the third focus in a specific situation, it may be less useful for a variety of situations over time. It tends to focus on the unique combination of factors affecting compliance in a specific instance. However, the kinds of questions addressed here concern a variety of instances for the organization. As such they focus on the general factor in the authority relationship. As used here authority will be that those in positions of responsibility in the organization and/or political system have sufficient expectation that their decisions are considered generally legitimate and will generally be willingly complied with by those to whom they are directed. To achieve this expectation the clients consider the decisions of the governors legitimate and generally acceptable, and hence authoritative for them.

The emphasis of this usage like those in category two above is on the general acceptance of authority by those who are subject to it. In the research presented here, the focus is on the students' view of the legitimacy of organization authorities, other political system authorities, and the political system itself.

With relationship to clients or citizens as well as with workers, authority is a neutral term. In itself it is not good nor bad. As stated in bureaucratic theory, authority potentially plays the role of enlisting the cooperation of organizational participants by overcoming their individual goals and getting them to engage in actions that further organizational goals. However, this salutary result depends on the exercise of authority and how it is received. And so it must be stated that in itself authority is not value loaded.

This point is especially relevant since in many writings and discussions authority has come to be confused with authoritarianism. Indeed, for many the term authority seems to have lost any meaning of its own in political organization and has come to be equated with authoritarian government. As Day (1963: 265) points out:

> Criticisms of "authority" in an authoritarian state is, therefore, frequently directed against coercive power unauthorized by the subjects and not really against authority at all . . . attacks on "authority" may often be attacks on what are more accurately called the unauthorized coercive power of governments. Authority and coercive power are so closely associated in some men's minds that one is often mistaken for the other.

This is to say that the presence of authority in government organizations does not imply either an excess of it or a misuse.

Negative evaluation of authority has come from two separate quarters, and both are based upon misunderstanding of the role of authority in organizations or government generally. First, to a certain extent this misunderstanding can be attributed to the work accomplished in the study of authoritarianism in psychological research. Popularly held conclusions from this research, but not related to it in any systematic way, have left the implicit assumption that authority in human relationships in general, and in government in particular, is somehow a manifestation of aberrant behavior and is something to be avoided. As Sartori (1965: 139) aptly states:

> For example, "authoritarianism" has suggested the epithet "authoritarian personality" to indicate the type of personality structure that is not adapted to the democratic way of life. The trouble is, again, that this term leaves the impression that the type of personality which can best serve democracy should be authority-less. Of course this is not so.

Authority then should not be confused with authoritarianism. The attitudinal relationship will be discussed in detail below.

A second area of criticism of authority has come from social scientists who in examining organizations have become concerned about the case where the expertise of the subordinate may be greater in some things than that of the superior. For example, Parsons (19xx) charges in his introduction to his translation of Weber's *Economy and Society* that Weber confused two types of authority in his discussion—the authority based upon technical competence and the authority based upon incumbency of a legally defined office. Parsons asserts there could be discrepancy between the two which often occurs. Perrow (1972) in his *Complex Organizations* analyzes the problem with considerable insight and points out that the distinction made by Parsons and invoked by so many since then fails to recognize the technical character of administration. Perrow (1972: 58) concludes:

> By assuming that official incumbency of a supervisory role has no relationship to expertise (expertise in management, in this case), it is possible for critics of the bureaucratic model to suggest a hiatus between expertise and occupancy of an official position. It was Weber's simple but enduring insight to see how crucial expertise was as a requirement for holding office throughout the hierarchy.

In the sense Weber delineates, authority is based upon expertise and, therefore, has the potential to motivate organization members toward organizational goals. For this potential to be realized, however, authority must be accepted by organizational participants, whether workers or clients, and influence their actions. Presumably if it is accepted, the organization will not be challenged.

AUTHORITY, CLIENTS, AND ORGANIZATION

This paper is concerned with behavior in organizations and the political system, and not with actual individual instances of compliance. The concern here is with a pattern of expectations these clients hold with respect to the making of decisions by those in governmental office. This pattern of expectations potentially has import for stress—within the organization, on the political system, and on the persistence of both. The research attempts to determine the nature of authority attitudes and whether they are significant for client behavior or whether other attitudes are more important.

Systems theory holds that the organization must be examined as a subsystem of its environmental system and attention must be given to how conditions and forces of the environment interact with various organizational subsystems that produce organizational activity. Johnson et al. (1973) list five primary subsystems of an organization for examination: organizational goals and values, the technical subsystem, the organization structure, the managerial subsystem, and the psychosocial subsystem. Organizational goals and values are taken from the broader sociocultural environment; the technical system involves the knowledge and techniques required for task performance; the organization structure is concerned with the ways in which the tasks of the organization are divided and with their coordination; the managerial subsystem spans the organization and relates organizational activities to its environment; and the psychosocial system consists of individual behavior and motivation, status and role relationships, group dynamics, and influence systems. Johnson et al. point out that obviously the psychosocial system is affected by external environmental forces as well as by internal ones. Thompson (1967) suggests that the essence of administration is found in understanding the basic configurations which exist between the various subsystems and the environment.

For public organizations, the environment plays an extremely central role for organizational activity. Thompson, among others, has pointed out that organizations desire to some extent to insulate themselves from their environments. For public organizations this is exceedingly difficult and generally held to be an improper goal. On the contrary, public organizations are created to be responsive to their environments. Public organizations are subsystems of the wider political system which places certain demands, provides supports, and interacts with organizational subsystems. The focus here is on the interactions of the political system with the managerial and psychosocial subsystems of the organization.

Specifically, the research seeks to examine the relationship between clients' attitudes and behavior, organizational authority, and the wider political system. It attempts to discover how such attitudes are determined and what their import may be for client behavior in the organization and the political system. Is the organization linked attitudinally to the political system with respect to organizational clients? Or is it separate and distinct? What is the nature of a linkage if it does exist? What is the significance for organizational activity? What is the significance of such client attitudes for the wider political system that constitute the relevant environment of the organization?

2. ENVIRONMENT OF UNIVERSITY ORGANIZATION

THE UNIVERSITY AS A SUBSYSTEM OF THE POLITICAL SYSTEM

Traditionally, the university as an organization has not been thought to be political in the same sense as a city or state government. However, in recent years observers have increasingly come to consider the university as a political subsystem. Easton (1957: 308), referring to the educational subsystem, notes that there are some kinds of social institutions whose actions are so heavily weighted with political consequences that they are considered political institutions. There are other kinds of institutions—

many of the actions of which have political consequences—that are primarily devoted to other aims. However, some of these have a considerable impact on the political system as a whole and, therefore, must be included in the political system. University organizations are receiving increasingly strong demands from their political environments for several reasons. Governments have increased their contributions through appropriations and grants-in-aid. The university has come to be regarded as a problem solver for diverse problems affecting society from space to health administration. The impact of these developments has not been lost on the public, and governments have been giving their demands an ever increasing hearing. As the universities have grown in commitment and complexity in response to such external inputs, internal interests have seemingly become increasingly politicized. Client demands for increased control of decision-making have been on the rise, and universities have been caught up in the nationalization of politics. Peterson (1969), in a study of several hundred college protests and the issues involved, came to the conclusion that protests over off-campus issues are more readily predictable than protests over campus conditions.

Thus, the university as an organization may usefully be examined as a subsystem of the political system. The task is to identify the nature of the interrelationships in terms of the organization's psychosocial system particularly with reference to its clients—the students. However, before focusing on client attitudes per se, it is necessary to discuss the nature of the political system itself.

UNIVERSITY ORGANIZATION—THE POLITICAL SYSTEM

Easton and Dennis (1969: 49) designate two conditions as the essential variables of any political system. "We will say that a political system persists when two conditions prevail: when its members are regularly able to allocate valued things, that is, make decisions; when they are able to get these allocations accepted as authoritative by most members most of the time." A given political system will not necessarily continue to persist under all environmental conditions. Indeed, political systems undergo varying degrees of stress. As Easton and Dennis state (1969: 52):

> The introduction of the notion of stress suggests that there may be forces at work that threaten to undermine the capacity of a society to sustain some kind of system through which values are authoritatively allocated. The persistence of some kind of political system would therefore depend upon the way in which it handles typical stresses.

One of the assumptions here is that conditions exist under which stress portends danger for the persistence of the political system or subsystem. This persistence is in question when the relevant members of the system or subsystem will be unable to make decisions regularly or, if they are able to do so, that they do not succeed in getting them accepted as authoritative by most members most of the time. Stress can be said to be a condition that occurs when disturbances—internal or external in origin—threaten to displace the essential variables of a political system beyond their normal range and toward some critical limit. Thereby stress prevents a political system from operating in a characteristic way.

One of the inputs for a political system is support. Stress may arise from the inability of a system to keep the input of support at some minimal level. Easton and Dennis (1969) state that support can be defined as feelings of trust, confidence, or affection that persons may direct at certain aspects of a political system. Support is necessary for system persistence and prosperity. It provides a context within which those in authority maximize their efficiency in making allocations. Major sources of stress can be found in the decline of support for any one of the following political objects:

The political community refers to that aspect of the political system that we can identify as a collection of persons who share a division of political labor.

The regime refers to that aspect of the political system that we may call its constitutional order in the very broadest sense of the term. Regime is used in a general sense to mean the political unit itself—its governing institutions, the general patterns of action, and the values that have been incorporated into the operation of government over time.

The authorities are those members of a system in whom the primary responsibility is lodged for taking care of the daily routines of a political system. In democratic systems we describe them as the elected representatives and other public officials, such as civil servants.

In terms of the university organization's wider political environment, the present study is concerned with the regime and authorities of the American political system. The linkage between these political objects and authority for the political system is under examination. Authority does not exist as some suprasocietal phenomenon. It must be invested in something finite. The authority of the American political system is invested in the regime or its constitutional order and its authorities or positions as defined above. Therefore, attention in the wider political environment must be directed to the legitimacy of authority of the regime (regime authority) and the legitimacy of authorities in official positions (position authority).

Individuals respond in a variety of ways to their government without knowing the particular officials involved in making the decisions. Legitimacy of the authority of the regime presumably provides additional support for particular political authorities. It theoretically provides a milieu of acceptance within which they can potentially operate.

In the American political system, authority is also invested in particular authorities or offices. As Hyneman (1968: 136) points out, an office is a lodgement of authority. Further, the distinction between a position and the man occupying it is fundamental to all modern states. Authority vests in the position not in the man. Legitimacy of position authority theoretically provides an incentive for the citizens to comply to directives. It is thought to be important for governmental decisions to be implemented.

According to Easton and Dennis (1969), the type of authority that a regime exercises may be distinguished by the degree to which its population acts in accord with regulations concerning the maintenance of the regime, and has diffuse orientations approving the regime and its authorities. This means in their terms it must receive compliance and support, with support being necessary for compliance.

Support may be divided into specific and diffuse. *Specific support* increases or declines depending upon the way in which the members interpret the consequences of the various outputs of the system. This will then be evaluated according to the various ideological positions of the populace. *Diffuse support*, on the other hand, is the generalized trust and confidence that members invest in the various objects of the system as ends in themselves. The peculiar quality of diffuse attachment is that it is not contingent on any quid pro quo as with specific support; it is offered unconditionally. Diffuse support represents a deep-rooted attachment to the political system that enables it to weather the discontent brought on by objectionable policies and by hardships members are called upon to undergo in the form of taxes, hazardous military service, or other sacrifices. For the political system to persist over time, presumably the politically relevant members must learn to put in a minimal level of diffuse support for the political objects.

It is difficult to determine exactly what this minimal level of diffuse support would be for any particular individual political system. Easton points out that even when those in authority positions are fully capable of making decisions and seeking to implement them, compliance on the part of the citizens will vary on a continuum. The probability of citizens accepting all the decisions of the authorities as binding is most assuredly going to be less than one. However, Easton (1965: 97) postulates that for persistence it must be higher than .5. Below this level the system would be in a state of constant turmoil and confusion. The ratio must fall within a limited range well above that of chance, because below that level the system would collapse for lack of sufficient authority being attached to its allocations.

Rose (1969) states that little attention has been given to the minimum level of mass support and compliance necessary to maintain a regime. It is possible that the withdrawal of support and compliance by a small number of people may produce a reaction out of all proportion to the number involved, because initiators of an insurrection depend for success upon the multiplier and demonstration effects of their behavior. It is not quite clear how large the small group of defectors must be in order to alter a regime's authority pattern substantially. The implication for the study of student behavior here is obvious.

The view taken here is that diffuse support for a political system is not a static phenomenon. Different groups may offer or withhold support at various times, and the degree of support for given populations will also vary. As stated above, support may be at any point on a continuum for a given time. The particular level is subject to change. For this reason, the authority of a political system must be considered as variable—not a constant. This perspective leads to the assessment of existing levels of support for authority at different times and the analysis of its meaning for client compliance.

Authority and Compliance

A useful perspective from which to view the function of authority in the operation of the organization is embodied in the concept of cost. The idea here is that under a given set of conditions, additional or fewer resources presumably will be required for organization authorities to make authoritative allocations, depending on the level of legitimacy attributed to the authority of the regime of the wider political system of which the organization is a part. Herein presumably lies the real value of the legitimacy of authority. As Dahl (1963: 32) reports:

> When a political system is widely accepted by its members as legitimate, and when the policies of its officials and other leaders are regarded as morally binding by its citizens, then the costs of compliance are low. Conversely, when legitimacy and authority are low, leaders must use more of their money, police, privileges, weapons, status, and other political resources to secure compliance.

One indication of the benefits of legitimacy of authority for the political system can be is pointed up by a study of strife conducted by Gurr (1968) for the years 1961-1963. A number of nations were identified that had less strife than might be expected on the basis of characteristics they shared with more strife-ridden nations. One apparent common denominator among them was a high degree of perceived popular legitimacy of the regime.

Specific support is the other variable that may have import for client compliance. As mentioned previously, specific support increases or declines depending upon the way in which the members interpret the consequences of the various outputs of the system. Attention for specific support is focused on ideological positions of the populace. As pointed out by Searing et al. (1973: 419) behavior resulting from specific support orientations are quid pro quo acts. Like diffuse support they are ultimately determined by favorable orientation toward institutions, but what distinguishes specific support behavior is its contingency upon client approval of the organization's policies.

During the period of considerable campus unrest, a number of issues involving Vietnam and right of dissent came under fire, especially by those considering themselves ideological liberals. It is possible, therefore, that these specific orientations rather than, or in addition to, more diffuse orientations toward the organization and political system legitimacy were responsible for absence of client compliance. To the degree that beliefs of this type are involved, a shifting of policies should be sufficient to obtain compliance. However, to the extent that more diffuse support orientations are involved, only actions which restore the legitimacy of authority of the organization and/or the political system will suffice.

A political system of course does not exist as a unitary entity. It is made up of various subsystems which are interrelated in a variety of ways. In the American political system there are different subsystems of the political system including federal, state, local, and—with regard to students—a university subsystem. Within these levels, there are different functional agencies and departments, or subsystems of the main subsystems. The citizen interacts with the political system at several points on the various levels and with the various agencies. His orientation toward the legitimacy of authority of the regime and the authorities as well as his ideology is developed through a combination of his perception and the actions of the relevant subsystems of authority.

In the American political system the subsystems are interrelated with the citizen through a nationalization of issue concerns that has taken place over time. This means that often issues or crises are focused into the national arena and then reverberate through the subsystems. The question here is: how do the subsystems of the political system interrelate with organizational subsystems in terms of clients?

UNIVERSITY ORGANIZATION–THE MANAGERIAL SUBSYTEM

The national political situation in the political system has not been without its impact on the university managerial subsystem. University administrators, as Epstein (1970) points out, are objectively not in a particularly strong authority position. However, students may perceive them as the responsible authority figures. To begin with the university authority system has been collegial rather than strictly hierarchical. The faculty shares in many of the relevant decisions that concern students. In addition, the authority of university administrators is constrained by the actions of state government and boards of trustees. The authority of the administration over their clients is constrained by various traditions and in recent times has been further pared back. The university managerial subsystem has been referred to as a system of multiple, crisscrossing authority–relations of differing types and strengths.

The authority of university administrators in the United States was increasingly challenged by activists as a part of their total protest program. Issues such as Cambodia, ROTC, and Dow Chemical led to challenges of academic authority and increased demands for governmental structural change in the university. Even demands for the alteration of the purposes of the university itself to "social action" were made.

The result of this had been considered by many observers to have undermined the authority of administrators–the holders of formal authority positions in the university managerial subsystem.

Many students may not perceive the administrators of universities as politically relevant. However, in crisis circumstances the actions of university authorities–as a result of issues in the wider political system–often meld with the actions of other governmental officials. Student sympathy for activists in crisis situations is well documented. At times governmental action can strike home hard, as in laws dealing with financial aid to university students.

The university provides an ideal setting for challenge to the political system. University authorities are available and vulnerable. Grievances are present and can be exploited. The ecological concentration of challenge activity can have maximum impact.

It might be expected that students in large residential university settings would be more affected by these conditions. In these the student spends most of his time with other students and "campus" concerns are more immediate to him than if he merely commuted to the campus, returning for classes, returning home to the concerns of family and friends not connected with the university. In the large university setting the individual's role as "student" may make him more cognizant of campus concerns including the large university population's concern with the larger political system. In short, situational components may accentuate feelings toward the political system and its subsystems. These will also be examined.

UNIVERSITY ORGANIZATION–THE PSYCHOSOCIAL SUBSYSTEM

As mentioned previously, the psychosocial subsystem of an organization consists of individual behavior and motivation, status and role relationships, group dynamics and influence systems. This paper is concerned with client attitudes with respect to the organizational authorities and the wider political system of which the organization is a part.

In the previous section, two types of support were discussed that were of significance—specific support and diffuse support. The question becomes: what are the client attitudinal referents for these types of support and what import do they have for client behavior?

Diffuse support is embodied in attitudes toward authority, and specific support is more involved with ideological attitudes. It will be useful to review these attitudinal components and suggest how they may be related to behavior relevant to the university organization.

Attitudes Toward Authority–Previous Formulations

One of the earliest studies dealing with the attitudinal component of political behavior of authority was *The Authoritarian Personality* by Adnorno et al. (1950). The authoritarian personality, as the Berkeley researchers conceived it, combines external social repression with internal repression of impulses. In order to achieve internalization of social control, the individual's attitude towards authority takes on an irrational aspect. The individual achieves his own social adjustment only by taking pleasure in obedience and subordination. The F-Scale was developed to test for the presence of the Authoritarian Syndrome. It consists of the eight dimensions of conventionalism—authoritarian submission, authoritarian aggression, anti-intraception, superstition and stereotype, power and toughness, destructiveness and cynicism, projectivity, and exaggerated concern with sexual goings-on. Various methodological criticisms have been made about the original study (Christie and Jahoda, 1954; Christie et al., 1958). However, Brown (1965) stated in an insightful review that in spite of several methodological defficiencies in the original and subsequent studies positive statistical interrelationships among the various dimensions seem to appear consistently.

Since the original authoritarian personality research, literally hundreds of studies have been completed to expand and improve on the propositions raised in that study. It appears now that the true authoritarian personality in its full form is to be found in but a small minority of people. However, it stems from the same process in which all individuals obtain their basic attitudes toward authority in general and political authority in particular.

Shils (1954) in his critique of the *Authoritarian Personality* proposes an extension of authoritarianism which is a right-wing phenomenon to a more generalized authoritarianism which may take on both left and right-wing forms. He charges the original design with the failure to distinguish between totalitarian Leninism, humanitarianism, and New Deal interventionism. Shils sees an overlap between right authoritarianism and the central features of Bolshevism. Both left and right authoritarianism are characterized by hostility toward parents; that of the right is expressed in the loyalty and submissiveness of the authoritarian personality and is a reaction formation against hostility toward his parents. The left authoritarian denies the authority of the state for the authority of the party. Sanford (1973: 169), an author of the original authoritarian personality study, has recently stated that "left-wing authoritarianism has so far been poorly conceived and investigated."

The basic problem with studies that have attempted to tap the attitudes of the left in terms of the authoritarian syndrome is that they are still looking for the basic positive, if irrational, attachment to a source of authority whether it be the state or party. However, this leaves another aspect of attitudes toward authority unexamined. Those who have a positive attachment to authority have been described. However, is the person at the low end of the F-Scale nonauthoritarian or is he possibly antiauthoritarian? The problem is that the absence of a positive authoritarian syndrome does not tell us anything about a possible negative attitudinal orientation toward authority. It is possible that negative attitudinal orientations may also be observed. For instance, Adorno et al. (1950: 772) stated in the original study:

> We encountered a few subjects who had been identified ideologically with some progressive movements such as the struggle for rights, for a long time, but with whom such ideas contained features of compulsiveness, even of a parnaoid obsession and who, with respect to many of our variables, especially rigidity and "total" thinking, could hardly be distinguished from some of our high extremes.

Thus, on the compulsive and there may be an antiauthoritarian attitudinal type.

Bay (1958: 206) proposes an antiauthoritarian type that may provide a starting point for discussion. In raising the question of antiauthoritarianism, Bay defines it as:

> A defensive predisposition to oppose uncritically standards and commands supported by authorities. The antiauthoritarian syndrome correspondingly is a group of attitudes tending to correlate highly with antiauthoritarianism. And the antiauthoritarian personality is a type of person characterized by this attitude syndrome.

Bay's antiauthoritarian displays an intolerance of ambiguity, both cognitively and affectively:

> He represses awareness of his own weakness and dependency needs. He sees all authorities as bad and wicked and all weak people as exploited and persecuted. He, too, is unable to tolerate the awareness of a complex, ambiguity-ridden world and unable to see the complexity of human motivations in himself and others.

A possible explanation for the acceptance and rejection of authority may be explicated here by reference to Mead's (1967) and Cooley's (1967) concepts of the "self" and the "significant other." In the concept of the self, the person has certain core values which he considers part of his self-concept as he views himself as an object. When he interacts with others, the person allows certain individuals to affect these core values and denies other individuals the right to affect them. When he comes in contact with others, the person compares what the other individual does and says with his core values and needs, and acts accordingly. If the other individual is considered significant by the person, his values may be altered if the actions of the other are divergent, or the values may be reinforced if they are congruent. The degree to which the individual allows others to alter these values is dependent upon the extent of his dependency on others to fulfill his needs. As stated, the antiauthoritarian has repressed his dependency needs so it is reasonable to propose that he will allow less alteration of his core values.

The antiauthoritarian, like the authoritarian, experiences great anxiety and cannot tolerate ambiguity that presents a challenge to his self-concept. For this reason his reactions are ego defensive.

The antiauthoritarian really has never been fully socialized to accept the authority of secondary authorities to tell him about his "self." Secondary authorities are those in authority positions who do not know him as an individual as do primary authorities such as parents or employers.

Behavior by secondary authorities that is counter to the antiauthoritarian's core values is automatically rejected because it is frustrating to him.

The result of this pattern, according to Bay (1958: 217), is that the antiauthoritarian sets up ingroups and outgroups for himself as readily as does the authoritarian. The outgroups for the antiauthoritarian are the secondary authorities who are likely to be precisely the ingroup for the authoritarian. Failure to reject outgroups categorically for both results in a great deal of anxiety due to their intolerance of ambiguity. The actions of secondary authorities are not evaluated on their own merits than—not separated in the cognitive or affective thinking of the antiauthoritarian. This thinking in relation to secondary sources is closed. This concept is crucial to more general attitudes toward authority and will be discussed below.

The secondary authorities are then defined by the antiauthoritarian as members of an aggressive outgroup. Bay (1958: 366) suggests the expression of hostilities by the antiauthoritarian further helps him to allay his anxiety.

Attitudes Toward Authority—A Reformulation

To this point the discussion has concerned the antiauthoritarian syndrome in its compulsive form to provide a balance to the well-known authoritarian syndrome replicated hundreds of times in research. The objective here is to illustrate the psychological field of attitudes toward authority. All dispositions toward authority are not of the compulsive type represented by the authoritarian and antiauthoritarian personalities. These represent processes somehow gone amiss. However, the authority formation process which all individuals undergo provides them with basic cognitive and affective orientations toward authority.

In light of the discussion above, it is preferable to conceive of affective orientations toward authority not in terms of discrete types but in terms of an attitudinal continuum. Depending upon the particular socialization experience which individuals undergo, and depending upon their evaluation of authority performance and impact on them, different points on the continuum will be occupied ranging from authoritarian, positive toward authority, neutral, negative toward authority, through antiauthoritarian.

It would seem much more fruitful to employ a continuum approach in describing populations with respect to their affective attitudes toward authority objects, whether the regime or authorities. Relying exclusively on explanations that account for compulsive types, whether authoritarian or antiauthoritarian, leaves a large part of any given population whether citizens or clients unexamined. The current research conceives of a distribution of authority attitudes toward both the regime and the authorities of the American political system. Data will be presented to explicate these distributions.

We have no evidence to indicate how a given population distributes on the continuum or how population distribution changes over time. It is not unreasonable to expect that some societal groups will be distributed more toward the positive pole while others are distributed toward the negative pole. Such a continuum represents the basic predispositions available. A given individual may be placed at any point on the continuum.

In addition, an individual's cognition of different authorities will affect various distributions of attitudes toward authority. In other words, individuals may group various authorities as being important for their attitudes in the organization or the political system at a given time. Later, how college students grouped certain authorities will be examined.

Socialization Toward Authority

An examination of the socialization of attitudes toward authority is relevant here. A major question for the organization is the origin of client authority attitudes and their susceptibility to change by action on the part of organizational authorities. There has been much controversy over the socialization or childrearing of those involved in campus protests and their dispositions toward authority. Specifically, as Halleck (1968) states, several have laid the cause of unrest on the middle-class family, saying permissive childrearing practices and/or a general permissiveness of the society are responsible for student attitudes that are disrespectful of authority. Bettleheim has asserted that male activists are the product of an inadequate socialization experience in the home. His idea is that the home life of male activists did not provide growing boys a chance to work through their Oedipal competition with the father. Thus, today's male activist assaults the constituted governmental authority as a way of working through unsettled relationships with authority.

This paper will explore the socialization of individuals toward authority; attention will be paid to theory and analysis of radical activist socialization. One line of research which has been directed at interviewing children has as its major tenet that childhood socialization experiences directly structure adult attitudes toward political objects. This line of research stresses the primacy principle—that those experiences learned first are most important for later behavior. The research stresses that the first socialization experiences which every individual undergoes are in relationship to his parents. The parents are responsible for the early learning experiences in all areas. They are also the first authority figures with which the child comes in contact. The Dubins (1963) state major areas of learned behavior, the authority inception period, extends from birth through the first six to ten years of life. During this period there is a progressive increase in the number and variety of behaviors covered by authority relations between the child and his parents. The initial acts of authority to which the child is subjected focus almost exclusively on his performance of physiological functions: successive experiences deal with control of himself, then relations with things, and finally relations with other people. The conflict between the desire to do exactly what the child wants and conformity to parental directives is somehow resolved during this period. The conflict is resolved by the imposition of parental authority throughout the authority inception period.

The argument is that parental imposition of authority on the child in complex social relations teaches him about the variable character of social demands on individual behavior and instructs him in the fact that there are ranges of acceptable behavior for almost all situations of action. In addition, through adjustment to authority the child has established for him, particularly through the authoritative acts of his parents, the fundamental concept of legitimacy. The imposition of parental authority is held to be fundamental to the establishment of normative judgments in the child as the crucial link between social order and the internalization of norms that preserve that order. Finally, authoritative parental behavior during the authority inception period lays the foundation for the child's future conception of the authoritative figure and is critical in providing him with a generalized image of an authority holder.

The child adopts or learns his values also, and the literature usually proposes that his primary values come from the parents. The child derives many of his political attitudes first from his parents and then from the school experience. Hess (1963: 545) stresses that anticipatory socialization of political orientations occurs long before adulthood and actual political behavior, and that the nature of this early conceptual and apperceptive experience influences subsequent socialization and behavior.

Easton and Dennis (1962) found that the groundwork for a high degree of positive diffuse support is laid during the political socialization process that the American child undergoes at an early age. Greenstein (1965) and also Hess and Torney (1967) found an extraordinarily high positive regard for the president and also for other political authorities such as the policeman.

Hess (1963: 546) found that the expression of highly positive attitudes toward the president is apparently not greatly influenced either by the incumbent of the office or by partisan affiliation. He claims that in the U.S.

the child is socialized into attitudes toward a role, that is, to a position of authority in the system, and not to the occupant of the office. Hess states that as the child grows to adulthood, he is exposed to considerable debate and conflict over the merits of alternative incumbents of the presidency and of other roles in the political structure. There is constant danger that criticism of the occupant will spill over to the role itself. He also found few differences between responses for governor and president, adding further evidence that the authority directive may be learned increasingly as a whole. After the initial early positive attachment to political figures, as institutions come more clearly into focus with advancing age, Hess and Torney (1967: 38) found that the overwhelming positive attachment to these figures was lessened.

The significance of this is presumably that as other values are learned from parents and others, discrepancies of behavior of political authority role occupants may lessen the legitimacy in the eyes of individuals possessing the diverging values and result in rejection of the authority of the authority holder. Greenstein (1965: 51) suggests that the greatest change away from political authority is probably during adolescence. This may be the beginning of the authority challenging period. Depending on the basic disposition acquired during the authority-inception period, challenges may be more or less overt for different individuals.

Other research would tend to call the structuring principle upon which the socialization studies are based into question. Searing et al. (1973) tested the "primacy" and "structuring" principles utilizing data from two national cross-section samples—the Survey Research Center's 1968 Election Study and the Southeast Regional Survey. The "primacy" principle involved in many socialization studies holds that early political learning is relatively enduring and the structuring principle holds that orientations acquired during childhood structure the later learning of specific issue beliefs. They found no support for either principle. Thus, if these principles do not hold among clients, the permissiveness hypothesis is also unlikely to hold.

Socialization of Student Activists

As mentioned previously, there has been much discussion of the backgrounds of those students participating in campus disturbances. Permissiveness in the home has been cited as a cause of unrest.

There has been some research that distinguishes the backgrounds of student activists from the less politically committed students. These studies (Flacks, 1967; Trent and Craise, 1967; Keniston, 1968; Watts and Whittaker, 1966) have shown that students involved in protest activities are characteristically from families that are urban, whose parents are highly educated with a disproportionate number of postgraduate degrees, more professional occupations, higher than average incomes, and from homes where formal religion is not important or Jewish. Flacks has concluded that unlike the campus radicals of the thirties, who were attracted to radicalism because they were economically deprived or because their economic mobility was blocked, the present student movement is predominantly composed of students who have been born to high social advantage and who are in a position to experience the career and status opportunities of the society without significant limitations. Greenstein (1965) holds that families with these characteristics are precisely the kind where permissive practices are likely to be followed. Flacks (1967) tests this notion in his study by administering the semantic differential to both students and their parents. Activists tend to rate their parents as "milder," "more lenient," and "less severe" than do nonactivists. Similar data was obtained from the parents. Looking at these data, the psychologists Jeanne Block, Norman Haas, and M. Brewster Smith (1968) conclude:

> Many young activists in contemporary America were reared under the influence of Benjamin Spock who, as an articulate pediatrician, led a revolt against the more authoritarian, rigid, constraining child-rearing practices. . . . It may be argued that the emergence of a dedicated, spontaneous generation concerned with humanitarian values and personal authenticity is a triumph of Spockian philosophy and principles. Others have suggested, in a less benign interpretation, that activism is the consequence of excessive parental permissiveness, a failure to teach respect for authority, and an unfortunate submission to the needs and feelings of the child.

Keniston (1968), in his study of young radicals, suggests that they were unable as children to express their hostility toward their parents but as adolescents can toward secondary authority figures.

Flacks and also Keniston claim that in fact, far from rejecting their parents' values, student activists desire to see them implemented. Their "gap" with their parents is that they see their parents as ineffectual in securing these important values in society. When activists see a discrepancy between the values their parents have taught them and their parents' inaction to implement them, they can repress their hostility against their permissive but ineffectual parents; but when they see a discrepancy between these values and the actions of public authority figures, their authority disposition, allows an expression of hostility toward the public figures. There is seemingly substantial data (Flack, 1967; Trent and Craise, 1967; Watts and Whitaker, 1966) to indicate that activists are drawn more heavily from the humanities and the social sciences.

Student Attitudes Toward the Legitimacy of Authority

The campus activist socialization literature suggests socialization experiences that may have led to negative orientations toward authority, that may have found ready outlets in the political arena, and that may have manifested themselves in overt and sometimes violent acts.

The outbreaks and the decline in the acceptance of the legitimacy of authority by college students may occur because of the interaction of their previous socialization experiences and the socialization experience of their college years. There is a growing body of theory that the American college student occupies a post-adolescent but preadult stage of life called "youth." Keniston (1968) suggests that the youth stage is made possible by college attendance which postpones entry into full sociological adulthood and contributes to an extension of the challenging of authority period. Individuals in this stage are not identified with their future professions but with their role of examining their basic relationship with existing society. According to this line of theory, what happens during "youth" is that the individual clarifies the relationship between self and society. The identification is not with the adult society but with others of the same life stage and their concerns.

The Legitimacy of Authority and Dissent

The connection between socialization toward authority and socialization of aggression has been discussed. Here the discussion is extended to authority and dissent.

One possibility is that as the legitimacy of authority for the regime and/or the authorities declines, the likelihood of noncompliance and thus support for overt methods of dissent increases. Gurr (1970: 185) suggests that the intensity and scope of normative justification for political violence vary strongly and inversely with the intensity and scope of regime legitimacy. However, feelings of legitimacy for the authority of the regime and its authorities may not be the only factor for the individual in deciding to engage in or support such acts. The feelings of legitimacy may be primary or contributory. If primary, specific issue concerns would not make much difference in the individual's decision to support or engage in overt methods of dissent. If contributory, the feelings of legitimacy of authority may provide an attitudinal background against which disagreement with particular policy decisions could spark actual participation or support for acts of dissent. In this paper, the nature of the relationship between student attitudes toward the legitimacy of authority of the regime and authorities of the American political system will be examined empirically.

Even if the authority hypothesis holds, a further question remains: is it a rejection of the regime of the political system as a whole or of the authority of those in particular positions that is important for behavior? Further, if it is the rejection of authorities in particular positions, are the attitudes of clients toward authorities in the organizational subsystems more controlling for compliance than those in other subsystems of the political system or not? That is, the literature on protest activists suggests that students generally would approve more overt acts of noncompliance than would the population as a whole. It is claimed that the university organization itself provides situational stresses and value discrepancies. Further, universities provide formal authorities which impose constraints. Either because of these imposed constraints or perhaps due to the nationalization of university concerns, holders of position authority in the university subsystem may be seen as representatives of authority of the larger society. The moderate student with these same attitudes may act as a reference group for more activist students and also constitutes a reservoir of potential noncompliance.

In other words, authorities in the university subsystem may be more relevant for their clients in relationship to the political system, because they perceived that this is where the authority structure has impact on them. The legitimacy of orgranizational authorities then may be the important variable for compliance or noncompliance. Alternatively, if compliance is more dependent on attitudes toward the authority of the regime as a whole or other authorities in the political system, the constraints on organizational authorities presumably increase.

Specific Support Ideology: An alternative line of explanation from that which looks to basic personality orientations arising out of particular socialization patterns would involve ideology of clients, or specific support orientations, rather than authority attitudes or diffuse support orientations. Specific support, it will be remembered, requires some quid pro quo as a condition for support.

During the period of substantial campus unrest, a number of varied issues received significant public as well as campus attention. Vietnam was an obvious issue, but there were many other issues both national and local in character of concern to university students. Civil rights, the draft, actions of law enforcement agencies, role of the university in society, educational policy, free speech, as well as many local issues were not just covered in mass media but were the topics of mass rallies, meetings, and considerable informal discussion. Some of these issues were subject to decision by university organizational authorities, while others were completely outside their purview. While it may be fruitful to examine the relationship between opinion and compliance on each individual issue, the range and mix of issues, including local ones, would make comparative analysis among organizations extremely difficult. Rather, it may be more useful to know the ideological orientation of clients that may have import for new issues that arise.

Ideology—Specific Support: As alluded to above, much of the student activist literature has pointed out that those participating in acts of protest or disruption have been liberal in their political orientations. In opposition to the authority hypothesis, client noncompliance may not be a result of a lack of diffuse support, but a result of a lack of specific support. The import of such a phenomena would be that organizational authorities may reasonably expect that issue changes would result in increased disposition among clients toward compliance; whereas under the authority hypothesis if the basic legitimacy of authority is absent, such issue changes presumably may not affect disposition toward compliance as readily.

While there has been some discussion about the usefulness of the liberal-conservative distinction, recent research has pointed out evidence of increasing applicability. Harris (1971: 410) has shown that substantial percentages of the general American public correctly perceived the conservative and liberal positions on various issues of the day. Data provided by Free and Cantril (1968: 220, 235) show that general public survey respondents are reasonably correct in their self-classification as liberals or conservatives in comparison with their issue preferences. According to Hero's (1969: 400) extensive analysis of historical poll data, by the late 1960s self-declared liberalism or conservatism had been almost as good a predictor of a person's civil rights views as of his social welfare opinions. Also, the use of ideological language increases among general public survey respondents when ideological differences in stimuli—in this case candidates—become magnified (Field and Anderson, 1969; Pierce, 1970). Finally, Axelrod (1967) found that opinions become increasingly correlated in conservatims-liberalism terms if one isolates the relatively informed segment of the public.

This research would suggest that for a more highly educated group—which college students presumably represent—and in situations where stimuli may take on strong ideological tones—which during the period of campus unrest could be reasonably characterized as occurring—liberalism-conservatism may be a very good summary variable to characterize specific support for the clientele group under examination. Further, validity—predictive validity—would be provided if it were shown to predict differences in dependent variables.

Therefore, a concern of this paper will be to determine the relative predictive power of this specific support attitude for noncompliance in relationship to diffuse support orientations.

3. FOCUS OF INQUIRY

This paper will test several alternative explanations for client disposition of compliance or noncompliance. One line of theory previously reviewed suggests that background factors involved in the individual's socialization experiences are determinant. This may be a direct relationship. However, a strong movement in this line of theory suggests that these socialization experiences structure orientations toward authority that in turn determine compliance/noncompliance. A question that is involved in testing this proposition becomes: are attitudes toward the authority of the regime of the political system, the constitutional order and rules of the game, important for compliance—or are attitudes toward those in specific authority positions in the political system or the organization more important for compliance?

A second line of theory hypothesizes that specific support orientations—ideology—may be controlling for compliance/noncompliance. This carries with it the implication that as issues change, in interaction with such orientations, compliance behavior is likely to change.

The theoretical discussion has centered on diffuse support for the American political system in terms of perceived legitimacy of regime authority and position authority in the political system. The empirical goals of this study are:

(1) to determine what structure of beliefs exists with regard to both the legitimacy of regime authority and position authority in the American political system;

(2) to determine the relative respondent support levels for noncompliance in the form of dissent, for example, having participated in various forms of dissent, supporting the participation of others, and willingness to engage in various forms of dissent in the future;

(3) to determine the extent of the relationship between certain background factors and both the postulated attitudinal antecedents of support for dissent actions and the dissent actions themselves; and

(4) to test multivariate models of the relationships between variables discussed above.

RESEARCH FOCUS–SPECIFICATION OF VARIABLES

One focus of the inquiry has centered on diffuse support for the American political system in terms of attitudes toward the legitimacy of regime authority and position authority. Regime, as stated above, refers to that aspect of the political system that is called its constitutional order in the very broadest sense of the term. This order includes not only the arrangement of offices and distribtion of powers but also the values both explicit and implicit in the constitutional order of society and the continuing means for implementing them. For example, representative government as a principle and the way congressmen are elected would be included. One may disagree with some practices incorporated within the regime, but to accept the legitimacy of its authority, the citizen must generally agree that it is the regime the community should have. The citizens then must generally accept it for all practical purposes as a whole for diffuse support to exist. When large segments of the community do not, stress is said to exist.

Some notion of the nature of stress in this regard is embodied in such current statements as "the system is breaking down" or "the system no longer works." These are references to the viability of the regime of the political system. The empirical task here is to measure attitudes toward the legitimacy of authority of the regime that imply this kind of situation. Low legitimacy of authority of the regime may be said to exist when individuals insist on radical change of the regime. When an individual says those principles embodied by the regime are no longer acceptable, then the regime may be said to have lost its legitimacy of authority for that individual. The widespread existence of radical attitudes of this type constitute low legitimacy and the widespread absence of radical attitudes of this type constitute high legitimacy for the regime.

Therefore, in order to examine the accepted level of the legitimacy of authority of the regime of the American political system, measure of attitudes calling for radical change of the regime will be employed.

The idea being tested is that college students as a client group have rejected the existing political system, or in the terms specified here, have denied the legitimacy of authority of the regime. By examining the relative presence of radical attitudes calling for a change of regime, the research will examine this commonly held idea with regard to the student sample presented here. Thus, *radical regime change attitudes* will be delineated.

The inquiry also concerns the legitimacy of position authority of those in the university organization and others in the American political system. As previously stated, the authorities are those members of a system in whom the primary responsibility is lodged for taking care of the daily routines of a political system. In the United States these are the elected representatives and other public officials, such as civil servants.

Rejection of the legitimacy of position authority in the organization and/or the political system may increase the costs of getting decisions accepted and leads to system stress. Under this line of reasoning for the governing process to function relatively smoothly, rejection of legitimacy of position authority must be kept to a minimum. Also, for those authorities where rejection of legitimacy of their authority is high, costs of governing will generally be high. That is, greater outlays of resources will be required to get their decisions implemented. Thus, *attitudes toward position authority* will be examined.

Further, the inquiry concerns the import of the specific support orientations of clients in terms of ideological predisposition for client behavior. Presumably, specific issues arising in interaction with this orientation can determine compliance/noncompliance.

Another focus of the inquiry is the structure of beliefs students hold with respect to position authorities. The various levels of government in the United States contain numerous authorities from president to city policeman. Students may respond to the legitimacy of their authority uniformly, randomly, or according to certain attitudinal criteria. As stated above, some evidence suggests that students do not respond to university authorities as members of the university, but also as representatives of the wider political community. To illustrate the structure of student beliefs with regard to the authorities of the American political system, the inquiry will include authorities of the national, state, city, and university subsystems who occupy various functional roles. An attempt will be made to delineate *the structure of student beliefs regarding organizational and system authorities.*

In addition, the inquiry looks at the structure of beliefs with respect to the regime of the American political system. While the items included with respect to the *regime* are not exhaustive of all possible aspects of regime authority, it is suggestive to examine the aspects included to uncover any attitudinal patterns that may be relevant.

The delineated structures of beliefs with respect to the legitimacy of regime authority and position authority in the American political system will also be subsequently useful in determining the relationship between attitudes toward authority and support for actions of dissent.

Another focus of the inquiry is determining the levels of student support for various actions of dissent. High support for strong actions of dissent creates stress for the organization and/or for the political system and increases costs of decision implementation to organizational authorities. High support for weaker actions of dissent may create less stress but still may increase costs of decision implementation. Alternatively, low support for actions of dissent implies low stress for the organization and low costs for authorities.

In this study, support for actions of dissent will be examined from three different standpoints:

(1) having participated in certain dissent actions (past participation),
(2) accepting others' participation in dissent actions (acceptance of participation), and
(3) willingness to possibly participate in such actions in the future (future participation).

By examining these three aspects an indication of the size of the dissent group, the reference group, and the potential dissent group for various actions will be revealed. Items concerning all three aspects will be included to assess levels of support for *actions of dissent.*

Another focus of this inquiry will be to examine the relationship of background characteristics with both attitudes toward authority and support for actions of dissent. Previously several background characteristics were discussed that other researchers and theorists have either found relevant or have postulated their relevance with regard to protest activities. These include permissiveness in childrearing, education of parents, income, grade point average, and academic major in the university. The first three refer to socialization experiences in the home and the last two refer to experiences within the university itself.

From the preceeding discussion, it would be expected that those coming from permissive childrearing experiences would generally possess more negative authority attitudes. These students should also come from higher income homes whose parents had more education. In addition, those who are generally the better students and who are majoring in the social sciences and the humanities should generally possess more negative authority attitudes. In addition, as noted earlier, it was learned that student activists who possessed these characteristics also were more ideologically liberal. It might be expected that these background variables that lead to more negative authority attitudes would also lead to ideological liberalism. This possible relationship will be examined. It is also possible that persons sharing these characteristics will be stronger supporters of actions of dissent without regard to the intervening attitudes. Specific hypotheses will be presented below.

MODELS

Based on the preceding discussion, it would be expected that feelings of low legitimacy toward the authorities and/or the regime of the political system would lead to higher support for actions of dissent in all three areas—participation, reference group membership, and willingness to participate in the future. Thus, the relationship between *radical regime change attitudes and also attitudes toward authorities with support for actions of dissent* will be examined. Alternatively as stated above, the primary reason clients may engage in protest is that they may feel that long-standing policies conflict with ideological positions they hold. It would be expected, then, that while it is possible for those holding conservative ideological orientations to perceive such value conflicts and thus engage in protest actions, that on the college campus such conflicts will be experienced most often by the ideological left. It would be expected, then, that those with liberal attitudes would manifest higher support for actions of dissent in the three areas. The relationship between *ideological attitudes* and *support for actions of dissent* will be examined.

Figure 1 illustrates the basic form of the hypothesized relationships between the variables in the study. The relationshps are presumed to operate in a causal fashion and are developmental in nature. The model takes the form of the developmental sequence where background variables affect attitudes toward ideology and authority which influence behavioral characteristics. The background variables include permissiveness in childrearing, education of parents, income, grade-point-average, and academic major. The attitudinal variables include ideological attitudes, regime radical change attitudes, and attitudes toward authorities. The behavior includes the acceptance of participation, past participation, and future participation.

The general causal ordering of the variables seems reasonable in that the background factors would seem to be prior to the attitudinal variables which would seem to be prior to the behavior variables. Analysis of the data indicates, though not conclusively, whether or not this model is applicable to the variables examined here. This ordering will be called the *developmental model*.

Another possible model is a direct causal sequence from the background variables to the behavioral variables indicating that any relationship found between the attitudinal variables and the behavioral variables is a spurious one. This model is illustrated in Figure 2. This would indicate

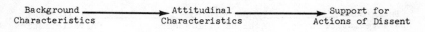

Figure 1: Developmental Model

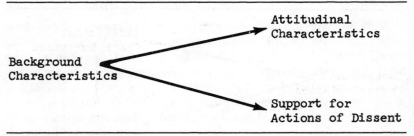

Figure 2: Spurious Model

the absence of a causal connection between the attitudinal variables and the behavioral variables, rather than that they are both caused by the background variables. This model would be inconsistent with the theoretical formulations heretofore discussed and a positive test of it would result in a necessary reformulation and retesting using different attitudinal variables. This ordering will be called the *spurious model.*

Still another possible model would be a causal sequence from the attitudinal variables to the behavioral variables and from the background variables to the behavioral variables, but none from the background variables to the attitudinal. This model is illustrated in Figure 3. This model suggests that people with the postulated attitudinal characteristics are indeed likely to engage in the postulated behavior but that these attitudes are not caused by the postulated background variables; and, in addition, people with the requisite background characteristics do not necessarily possess these attitudinal characteristics. This model indicates that either the attitudinal variables are caused by another set of background experiences, or that people undergoing a variety of socialization experiences may arrive with these attitudinal predispositions. A variety of alternate reformulations would need to be tested. This will be called the *independence model.*

A final model would be where the behavioral variables are the result of two forces, both of which originate in the background variables. One is transmitted through the intervening attitudinal variables and the other appears as a direct effect of the background variables because any additional relevant intervening attitudinal variables have been ignored. This model is Figure 4. In this case the relevant attitudinal sequence would have been revealed, and additional attitudinal variables that might conform to a

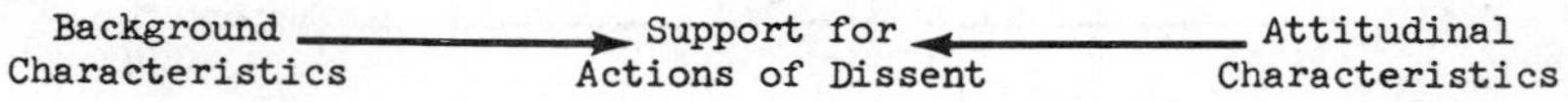

Background ⟶ Support for ⟵ Attitudinal
Characteristics ⟶ Actions of Dissent ⟵ Characteristics

Figure 3: Independence Model

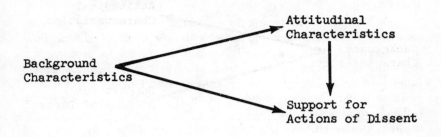

Figure 4: Hybrid Model

developmental sequence would have to be sought. This will be called the *hybrid model.*

In review, the evidence and theoretical formulations that have been considered suggest four primary models which have relevance to the concerns of this study:

(1) the developmental model calls for a developmental sequence of the three types of variables as discussed;

(2) the spurious model calls for no relationship between the attitudinal and behavioral variables;

(3) the independence model calls for a connection between the attitudinal variables and the behavioral variables independent of the connection of the background characteristics to the behavioral variables;

(4) the hybrid model calls for effects on the behavioral variables from both the attitudinal and the background variables with the attitudinal effect as part of a developmental sequence originating in the background experience; it is thus a hybrid of the first two.

OPERATIONALIZATION OF VARIABLES

As stated earlier, to examine attitudes toward the legitimacy of authority of the regime of the American political system it is necessary to examine regime radical change attitudes or radical attitudes calling for a change of regime. This attitudinal set was tapped by utilizing eight item statements from Christie's (1969) scale of radical attitudes. They are of the Likert type with possible responses including "agree strongly," "agree," "undecided," "disagree," and "disagree strongly" in that order. Items 1 and 3-8 are scored in this order from 1 to 5 with "agree strongly" scored 1, meaning high on radical change, and "disagree strongly" scored 5, meaning low on radical change. Item 2 was scored during coding with "disagree strongly" scored 1, meaning high on radical change, and "agree strongly" scored 5, meaning low on radical change.

These items express a feeling for fundamental change. In the questionnaire itself these items appeared mixed with other scale items, some positively worded and some negatively worded, to control for response set. Reliability of the scale will be discussed along with the structure of beliefs with regard to radical regime change in the next section.

Those holding position authority in the organization and the political system authorities were defined as those members of a system in whom the primary responsibility is lodged for taking care of the daily routines of a political system, which in the United States are the elected representatives and appointed public officials. Respondent attitudes toward the legitimacy of position authority was operationalized by means of the following procedure. Authorities from the four subsystems were included: the national subsystem, state subsystem, city subsystem, and university organization subsystem. In addition, authorities for each subsystem were included according to six functional responsibilities. They are chief executive, legislative, judicial, bureaucratic, prosecuting, and police.

The question asked was:

All of the following are in positions of authority in the United States in one way or another and make decisions that affect people in their respective areas. Different people think that some of them exercise legitimate authority and others do not. Some think all are legitimate, some think none are. Check those whose authority you consider not legitimate to make decisions that could or do affect you.

Asking the question in this way tests directly the perceived legitimacy of authority of each individual authority.

There is no presumption here that this categorization is meaningful in attitudinal terms for respondents. The structure of beliefs with regard to these authorities will be examined empirically. This categorization was employed to avoid bias by inclusion.

Checking of an authority by a respondent means, then, a rejection of the legitimacy of authority of that specific authority for that respondent.

Ideological attitudes are examined by reference to the respondent's characterization of himself in ideological terms as either a liberal or conservative.

Liberalism-conservatism was tapped here by asking, "Do you consider yourself to be liberal or conservative in politics?" Respondents refusing to pick either choice were classified as "neither."

As mentioned above, three aspects of support for actions of dissent—past participation, acceptance of participation, and future participation—will be examined.

The actions of dissent involved were talking to others to gain support for a position on a campus political issue, signing a petition of protest, picketing, participating in a sit-in, engaging in civil disobedience, and engaging in acts that destroy property. Acceptance of these types of actions on the part of others was measured in a slightly different manner than was the respondent's own participation. This was done to allow for the collection of additional information relevant to this question.

Respondents were given a "hand card" on which to mark their responses. It is reproduced in Table 1.

This question allows a determination of the most and least legitimate actions of dissent as perceived by the respondents as well as a region of acceptance by indicating how far down the scale the +'s extend and a region of rejection by indicating how far up the scale the —'s extend.

In order to assess the extent of respondent participation and willingness to participate in various actions of dissent, they were asked, "Have you ever?" Each act was then read in turn by the interviewer and the response affirmative or negative recorded. Then the respondent was asked for those same things, "Would you ever?" and again affirmative or negative responses were recorded. The actions were mixed with other forms of campus political participation. The items of interest to us here are presented in Table 2 in the order of their presentation in the interview schedule.

The background variables were operationalized as follows: permissiveness in childrearing was operationalized by degree of stress the parents of the respondent placed on obedience as perceived by the respondent. The scale utilized is a modification of the one developed by Kenneth P. Langton (1969: 25) in his study of family influence and adolescent political attitudes in the Carribean (see Table 3). The addition of the no-stress option (response 5) provides for an equal balance between high and low stress on obedience with option three providing the middle response. Respondents were asked, "As you were growing up how much did your parents stress obedience?"

Methodological Notes and Representativeness of Samples

The source of data for this study is an interview schedule which was administered to random samples of students on five campuses of Indiana University during the latter portion of the spring semester of 1970. The campuses from which the samples were drawn were Bloomington, Fort Wayne, Northwest at Gary, South Bend, and Kokomo. The mix of campuses allows for situational control and comparison in terms of campus type and size. Campus I, the Bloomington campus, is a large residential

TABLE 1
Dissent Actions Scale

Here are actions some students on college campuses have taken to present their grievances about such things as student participation in school politics, tuition raises, R.O.T.C. and civil rights. Mark with the following signs as indicated: HAND CARD--RESPONDENT MARKS OWN ANSWERS

A double plus (++) the one action you consider most legitimate for these students to engage in. (Use (++) only once.)

A single plus (+) other actions you consider legitimate for these students to engage in.

A double minus (--) the one action you consider least legitimate for these students to engage in. (Use (--) only once.)

A single minus (-) other actions you consider not legitimate for these students to engage in.

Mark each blank:

_____1. Talking to others to gain support for a position.

_____2. Signing a petition.

_____3. Picketing.

_____4. Sitting-in.

_____5. Engaging in civil disobedience such as taking a building.

_____6. Burning record files.

university with extensive undergraduate and graduate programs and a cosmopolitan client population of some 30,000. The other campuses are smaller, ranging in size from 2,500 to 8,000, and are commuter campuses. They are located in various parts of the state that are quite diverse in terms of industrialization and historical, political, and cultural background.

TABLE 2
Participation in Actions of Dissent

_____ Talked to others to gain support for a position on a campus political issue.

_____ Signed a petition of protest.

_____ Picketed.

_____ Sat-in.

_____ Engaged in civil disobedience.

_____ Engaged in acts that destroy property to achieve a goal.

The total number of students drawn in the random samples and the response rates are shown in Table 4.

Although the return percentages reported are uneven, the number of responses for each campus and the total sample is sufficiently high. In addition, the representativeness of the sample as judged by distribution of class and sex was checked and is considered acceptable. Very small deviations were evident. Representativeness for a sample means that the responses are not peculiar to a particular set of persons within the original sample.

TABLE 3
Permissiveness Scale

High   1. Parents demanded obedience at all times.

       2. Parents stressed obedience a great deal.

       3. Parents stressed obedience but allowed lots of leeway.

       4. Parents didn't stress obedience much; they allowed me to do pretty much what I wanted.

Low   5. Parents didn't care about obedience; I almost always did what I wanted.

TABLE 4
Samples and Response Rates

	Sample	Response	Rate
Campus I - Bloomington	556	172	30.9
Campus II - Fort Wayne	498	336	67.5
Campus III - Northwest	507	204	40.2
Campus IV - South Bend	496	212	42.8
Campus V - Kokomo	436	177	40.6
TOTAL	2493	1101	44.5

However, as suggested by McCloskey (1969: 4), requirements for sampling and for response percentages are fundamentally different depending upon the purpose of the inquiry. Discussing some basic tenets of survey research, McCloskey says, "In general, a sample must more perfectly reflect the characteristics of the universe being studied if the investigator wishes to describe that universe than if his main concern is to discover or test relationships among variables." In view of the representativeness of the sample and the over-riding research motive of attempting to test the relationship between variables, the sample is an adequate one for a fair testing of the hypotheses.

The interview schedules were administered by trained interviewers from each individual campus. The interviewing was conducted from April 10 to May 30 of 1970 at a time when instances of campus demonstrations aimed at various issues were widespread throughout the United States. Campuses I, III, and IV had all experienced some form of student demonstrations at some point prior to the administration of the survey.

4. FINDINGS

In terms of background characteristics, there were no significant differences between the campus sample populations with respect to sex or race. Significant differences were found with respect to income and education of father and mother for respondents from Campus I—the large university campus—with somewhat higher incomes and parental education found for students here. A family characteristic of significant concern was broadly termed "permissiveness," operationalized here as stress on obedience. As shown in Table 5, very few of the respondents perceived their parents as placing little stress on obedience, with only 8% of the total sample reporting that their parents did not stress obedience much or didn't care about it. On the other hand, few respondents felt they came from homes where obedience was demanded at all times (14%). The largest response was for the situation where parents stressed obedience a great deal or stressed it but allowed lots of leeway. Campus I respondents reported permissive experiences somewhat more frequently, although the majority here too reported that obedience was stressed to some extent.

The responses to the eight item scale used to operationalize radical regime change in order to reveal this aspect of authority orientations is found in Table 6. Average scale scores were determined for individuals by assigning 1 for an "agree strongly" response, 2 for "agree," and so on. A perfect radical regime change score would thus be 8, and a complete absence of radical regime change disposition would be 40. Scale reliability

TABLE 5
Permissiveness

Obedience*	Campus I	Campus II	Campus III	Campus IV	Campus V	Total
Demanded	17 (9.9)	40 (12.1)	40 (19.0)	26 (12.9)	30 (17.3)	153 (14.1)
Stressed	60 (34.9)	157 (47.6)	100 (47.6)	101 (50.2)	80 (46.2)	498 (45.9)
Allowed Leeway	72 (41.9)	115 (34.8)	58 (27.6)	53 (26.4)	51 (29.5)	349 (32.1)
Not Stressed	21 (12.2)	17 (5.2)	12 (5.7)	18 (9.0)	12 (6.9)	80 (7.4)
None	2 (1.2)	1 (.3)	0 (0.0)	3 (1.5)	0 (0.0)	6 (.6)
	172 (100.0)	330 (100.0)	210 (100.0)	201 (100.0)	173 (100.0)	1056 (100.0)

*Chi-square difference at .01 level.

TABLE 6
Radical Regime Change Score Totals

	Campus I	Campus II	Campus III	Campus IV	Campus V	Total
8–16	6	4	7	1	4	22
	(3.5)	(1.2)	(3.3)	(.5)	(2.2)	(2.0)
17–22	33	41	34	21	24	153
	(19.1)	(12.2)	(16.0)	(10.2)	(13.3)	(13.8)
23–28	88	160	102	88	84	552
	(50.9)	(47.6)	(47.9)	(42.9)	(46.7)	(47.2)
29–34	42	111	59	84	60	356
	(24.3)	(33.0)	(27.7)	(41.0)	(33.3)	(32.2)
35–40	4	20	11	11	8	54
	(2.3)	(6.0)	(5.2)	(5.4)	(4.4)	(4.9)
	173	336	213	205	180	1107
	(100.0)	(100.0)	(100.0)	(100.0)	(100.0)	(100.0)

was determined utilizing T ratios to measure the ability of each item to differentiate between the 25% of the respondents with the highest scale scores and the 25% with the lowest. In addition, item-to-scale correlation coefficients (Pearson's product moment correlation coefficient) were also computed. All measures for all scale items were statistically significant at the .01 level or higher confirming scale reliability. The dominant tendency is one of support for the regime, although there is some significant support for radical regime change.

As mentioned, respondents were asked to designate those formal offices from several functional categories of the organization and its political system whose legitimacy to make decisions about them they reject. The results appear in Table 7. Positions have been arranged from most to least legitimacy according to total sample responses.

The table reveals a diversity of acceptance of the legitimacy of position authority for organizational authorities and other political system authorities. For the total sample of respondents, rejection of legitimacy ranges from a low of 8.1% to a high of 48.8%. This diversity of range is consistent among the different campuses. The President of the United States undergoes the smallest rate of rejection. This finding may attest to the preeminent position of the presidency in the American system. In addition, this finding is interesting in light of several socialization studies which have found that in childhood the individual's first awareness of the political system is through personal attachment to the president, an attach-

TABLE 7
Rejection of Legitimacy of Authorities

	U.S. President	U.S. Congressman**	Governor*	State Legislator**	U.S. Supreme Court**	University President**	State Court of Appeals**	U.S. Attorney General	Dean of Students*	City Court Judge**	District Attorney	Mayor
Campus I	22 / 12.9	21 / 12.9	25 / 14.7	22 / 12.9	25 / 14.7	29 / 17.0	30 / 17.9	27 / 15.8	35 / 21.1	39 / 22.7	32 / 18.6	36 / 21.1
Campus II	29 / 8.8	29 / 9.1	35 / 10.7	35 / 10.6	36 / 11.1	41 / 12.3	39 / 11.9	42 / 12.8	41 / 12.8	43 / 13.0	44 / 13.3	59 / 18.0
Campus III	14 / 6.7	23 / 11.2	16 / 7.6	23 / 11.0	26 / 12.3	16 / 7.7	22 / 10.4	22 / 10.4	34 / 16.2	26 / 12.3	34 / 16.2	27 / 12.8
Campus IV	14 / 7.0	16 / 8.0	17 / 8.4	16 / 7.9	15 / 7.5	17 / 8.5	24 / 11.9	27 / 13.4	20 / 10.0	23 / 11.4	34 / 16.8	25 / 12.4
Campus V	9 / 5.1	6 / 3.4	7 / 3.9	7 / 3.9	9 / 5.1	14 / 7.8	11 / 6.1	14 / 7.9	14 / 8.0	23 / 12.8	19 / 10.6	23 / 12.8
Total	88 / 8.1	95 / 8.9	100 / 9.2	103 / 9.4	111 / 10.2	117 / 10.7	126 / 11.6	132 / 12.1	144 / 13.4	859 / 14.1	163 / 14.9	170 / 15.6

*Chi-square differences significant at the .01 level.
**Chi-square differences significant at the .05 level.

TABLE 7
Rejection of Legitimacy of Authorities (Continued)

	State Attorney General*	City Policeman	State Highway Patrol*	City Council	Campus Safety*	University Conduct Hearing Office*	Faculty Officer	Dean of Men	City Manager	Director State Alcohol Control Board	FBI Agent*	Director Selective Service
Campus I	44 26.5	41 24.3	49 39.0	52 31.5	64 37.9	62 36.3	51 30.4	70 41.4	71 41.5	77 44.5	89 52.4	95 55.6
Campus II	50 15.6	64 19.3	83 25.3	79 23.9	77 23.3	89 27.1	91 28.0	106 32.3	134 40.7	141 42.6	163 49.4	160 49.2
Campus III	31 14.8	34 16.2	46 22.1	52 24.8	50 24.2	59 28.1	61 29.0	80 37.9	74 35.1	86 40.6	90 42.9	100 41.8
Campus IV	34 16.9	35 17.4	51 25.5	42 21.0	47 23.4	40 20.0	45 22.4	61 30.3	66 32.7	85 42.3	91 45.0	97 48.5
Campus V	18 10.2	22 12.3	24 13.6	35 19.6	27 15.1	35 19.7	39 22.0	60 33.5	56 31.3	59 33.0	50 27.9	77 43.3
Total	177 16.5	196 18.0	253 23.4	260 24.0	265 24.4	285 26.2	287 26.5	377 34.7	401 36.7	448 40.9	483 44.3	529 48.8

*Chi-square differences significant at the .01 level.
**Chi-square differences significant at the .05 level.

ment which carries with it a tremendous positive affective attitude toward the president. Other offices are seen less clearly and have less positive affect.

It is generally suggested (Hess and Torney, 1967; Greenstein, 1965) that as the individual gets older, the positive affective personal orientation declines as institutions come more clearly into focus. However, the singular position of the president in the minds of individuals may never quite decline. One explanation possible here is that the position of the presidency reinforces the original singular orientation of the individual and continues to solidify the legitimacy of his authority. Representatives of the two other branches of the national government, congressmen and supreme court judges, also placed high on legitimacy of authority and are second and fifth respectively overall with slight deviations among campuses.

Two top state offices, governor and state legislator, are third and fourth respectively. The high authority of the university organization, the president, does very well also and is sixth overall. These top authorities are very close in the percentage of acceptance of their legitimacy. The decline in legitimacy across the table is gradual rather than precipitous. At the low end, from lowest to next to lowest, we find director of the Selective Service, F.B.I. agent, and director of the state alcohol board with 48.4%, 44.3%, and 40.9% rejection respectively.

Generally, a slightly higher percentage of Campus I respondents and a slightly lower percentage of Campus II respondents reject the legitimacy of the authorities presented here. On the whole, the similarities seem greater than the differences. The differences are ones of degree not in overall orientation. With but two exceptions for Campus I, the legitimacy of all authorities is accepted by a majority of students. The picture presented here is not one of high acceptance of legitimacy on one campus and high rejection on another, but one of difference in degree of acceptance. The implication of the table is that there is a diversity of legitimacy among authorities on the part of the respondents, ranging from overwhelming acceptance for some authorities to substantial rejection for others.

Structure of Beliefs

As mentioned previously, this study focuses on the structure of student beliefs regarding the regime and system authorities. With regard to both centers of authority, the examination is looking for additional patterns that suggest how students respond to authority. To identify these attitudinal patterns the data will be reduced to fewer indices that have theoretical import. The items for both the authorities and the regime of the American political system will be employed to develop indices of authority.

A technique for data reduction and index construction that will allow the determination of the dimensions of authority involved here is factor analysis. Factor analysis is a useful technique for empirically classifying variables on the basis of interdependency among the variables. However, the approach used in evaluating the results of the factor analysis is to attempt to relate it to the theoretical rationale used in the selection of variables. As Armstrong (1967) points out, if no theoretical framework is used to guide the selection of variables to be empirically classified, the resulting factor analysis would be meaningless. Since the interest here is to develop indicies of the legitimacy of authorities and one of radical change of regime, only variables that fit the theory have been selected. For authorities only positions representing major subsystem and functional referents have been chosen, and for radical regime change only statements calling for deviations from system norms have been included. The factor analysis results are more easily interpretable because the theoretical framework defines the boundaries within which the interpretation can take place.

Principal components factor analysis with varimax orthogonal rotation was chosen to examine data for both centers of authority.[1]

The factor analysis for the authorities of the American political system will be presented first. The analysis will seek to determine which authorities group and to see if the previous criteria for selection are relevant and to what degree. Application of the factor analysis to the 24 items yielded five dimensions of authority for system authorities. The factor loadings for the five factors are found in Table 8.

The first factor and the one that is most important in terms of the total variance explained is labeled the general authority factor. It is so labeled because general authorities for all system levels and functional classifications load highly on this factor. Those authorities having their highest loadings on the general authority factor include state legislator, city court judge, congressman, state attorney general, president of the United States, state court of appeals judge, and district attorney. Two others have relatively high loadings—mayor and university president. All load positively. High factor scores based on this factor indicate rejection of the legitimacy of these general authorities of the American political system.

The second factor is termed the bureaucratic authority factor because the three authorities that have their highest loadings on this factor are all administrative department heads from three different subsystems. They

TABLE 8
Rotated Loadings of Authorities Variables on Five Principal Factors

Variable Name	General Authority	Bureaucratic Authority	Organizational Authority	Police Authority	City Authority
Mayor	.441	-.072	.159	.124	.588
State Legislator	.677	_.101	.341	.024	.160
FBI Agent	.063	.385	-.029	.518	.217
City Court Judge	.489	.162	.033	.309	.305
Director State Alcohol Control Board	.074	.586	.002	.283	.263
U.S. Congressman	.724	-.096	.258	.005	.130
Dean of Students	.299	.190	.671	.047	.013
State Attorney General	.672	.286	-.064	.154	.115
U.S. Supreme Court	.721	.110	.073	.098	.034
Faculty Council Member	-.081	.176	.604	.113	.321
Director of Selective Service	.069	.588	.145	.110	.076
Governor	.647	-.107	.365	.054	.180
City Manager	.095	.258	.065	.121	.746
University Conduct Hearing Officer	.102	.450	.467	.276	-.006
U.S. Attorney General	.734	.267	-.005	.150	.073
University President	.429	.124	.559	.100	.079
City Councilman	.238	.065	.141	.090	.741
State Highway Patrolman	.266	.087	.043	.791	.059
Dean of Men	.126	.648	.285	-.165	-.019
President of U.S.	.687	-.059	.279	.109	.112
State Court of Appeals Judge	.644	.253	-.013	.264	.082
Campus Safety Patrolman	.012	.086	.470	.648	.072
District Attorney	.526	.284	-.065	.299	.186
City Policeman	.295	-.010	.153	.755	.118
Percentage Variance Explained	.211	.084	.090	.103	.081

are director of the state alcohol control board, director of the selective service, and dean of men. University conduct hearing officer also has a relatively high loading on the bureaucratic authority factor. High factor scores based on this factor for a respondent indicate a rejection of the legitimacy of bureaucratic authority in the political system.

The third factor is labeled the organizational authority factor because all four system authorities who have their highest loading on this factor are officials of the university organizational subsystem. They include dean of students, faculty council member, university conduct hearing officer, and university president. Campus safety patrolman also loads relatively high on this factor.

Notice, however, that four of the five university authorities load highly on three factors other than university authority. University conduct hearing officer loads highly on bureaucratic authority; university president highly on general authority; campus safety patrolman loads highest on police authority; and, dean of men loads highest on bureaucratic authority. This indicates that students responded to universities as representatives of the university organizational subsystem as well as in terms of their other orientations toward authority. A high student factor score on the organizational authority factor indicates a rejection of the legitimacy of the authority of university authorities.

The fourth factor is the police authority factor because those authorities engaged in the police function from all four system levels load highest on this factor. They are F.B.I. agent, state highway patrolman, city policeman, and campus safety patrolman. All load positively. High factor scores on this factor indicate a rejection of the legitimacy of police authority of the American political system.

The final factor is that of city authority. It is so named because all three authorities loading highly on this factor are officials of the urban subsystem of the political system. They include the mayor, city manager, and city councilman, which all have positive loadings. High factor scores on the city authority factor indicates a rejection of the legitimacy of authority of city authorities.

Students in the sample did not respond to the authority of officials of the political system in a random manner. Neither did they respond to them purely along subsystem or functional lines. Rather, they seem to respond to a general authority dimension including authorities from all subsystems and functions and then to functions and subsystems that may be relevant to specific interests or perceptions. Two of the factors involved functional authority and two involved subsystem authority.

The overall picture that emerges with respect to student perception of the legitimacy of authority of the authorities is a mixed one. On the one hand, legitimacy is not universally accepted; but on the other hand, it is not universally rejected either. The general situation seems to be one of a diversity of acceptance and rejection among students leaving some system authorities in an uncertain, if not challenged situation, while others are in a fairly secure position. The level of support thus varies a great deal for these authorities.

As previously stated, the structure of student beliefs with regard to the regime of the American political system is also of interest. The objective here is to see if there is more than one dimension of student response to the legitimacy of authority of the regime. Application of the factor analysis procedure to the eight items of the radical regime change scale yielded two dimensions of radical regime change. The factor loadings for the two factors are found in Table 9.

The factor that is most important in terms of the total variance explained is the institutional regime authority factor. It is so labeled because the items that load highest on this factor seem to pertain to orientations toward institutionalized conditions of the political system. Items one, three, four, five, six, and eight load highly on this factor. Low factor scores based on this factor indicate rejection of the institutional authority of the regime of the political system.

The second factor is the process regime authority factor. It is so labeled because the items that have their highest loadings on this factor pertain to orientations toward the process by which change is brought about within the political system. Items two, four, and seven load highly on this factor. As on the other, low factor scores on this factor constitute rejection of the process authority of the regime of the political system. One item, number four, loads highly on both factors, probably because it refers to process and institutional condition.

The factor analysis suggests that the students respond to the legitimacy of authority of the regime in terms of orientations to its institutions and processes for change. In subsequent analysis the relationship of both to support for actions of dissent will be examined.

As with perception of authorities, the percention of the legitimacy of the regime is diverse among respondents if not among campuses. Some respondents show considerable rejection of the regime, but on the whole there is considerable support for the regime of the American political

TABLE 9
Rotated Factor Loadings of Items

		Institutional Regime Authority	Process Regime Authority
1.	"The Establishment" unfairly controls every aspect of our lives; we can never be free until we are rid of it.	.560	.464
2.	There are legitimate channels for reform which must be exhausted before attempting disruption.	-.158	.799
3.	The United States needs a complete restructuring of its basic institutions.	.695	.181
4.	Authorities must be put into an intolerable position so they will be forced to respond with repression and thus show their illegitimacy.	.502	.549
5.	Even though institutions have worked well in the past, they must be destroyed if they are not effective now.	.597	.227
6.	A problem with most older people is that they have learned to accept society as it is, not as it should be.	.711	.120
7.	The streets are a more appropriate medium for change in our society than printing presses.	.233	.557
8.	Real participatory democracy should be the basis for a new society.	.648	-.268
	Percentage Variance Explained	.301	.204

system. These findings are similar to those of a 1970 nationwide survey among college students conducted by Louis Harris and Associates. When asked, "What kinds of changes in the system do you feel may be necessary to improve the quality of live in America?" 23% responded change in government or change in government structure. The largest response was

39% for change in people's attitudes. Change in regime, while being suggested by a good-sized minority, is by no means the conclusion of the clients as a whole.

Ideology

Another focus of inquiry in this study is the distribution of ideological attitudes in terms of liberalism-conservatism. The distribution of ideological attitudes is found in Table 10.

As might have been expected, students as a whole more readily classified themselves as liberals than conservatives. As previously stated, many issue areas may be covered in such a classification. The differences among the campuses are significant at the .01 level by chi-square test. Students from Campus I were more likely to typify themselves as liberals than as conservatives. In addition, they were more likely to classify themselves as neither conservative nor liberal than were respondents on the other campuses. Students on Campus III have the highest percentage designating themselves conservatives with 44.4%, and Campus V is second with 40.3%.

The nationwide Harris poll asked the following question: "On most issues, do you consider yourself far right, conservative, middle-of-the-road,

TABLE 10
Distribution of Ideological Attitudes

	Liberal	Conservative	Neither	
Campus I	99 (59.3)	34 (20.4)	34 (20.4)	167 (100.0)
Campus II	182 (54.8)	117 (35.2)	33 (9.9)	332 (100.0)
Campus III	106 (50.5)	73 (34.8)	31 (14.8)	210 (100.0)
Campus IV	101 (50.2)	81 (40.3)	19 (9.5)	201 (100.0)
Campus V	89 (50.0)	79 (44.4)	10 (5.6)	178 (100.0)
Total	577 (53.0)	384 (35.3)	127 (11.7)	1088 (100.0)

liberal, or far left?" For sake of comparison with these data the grouped responses were far left and liberal, 52%; far right and conservative, 17%; and middle-of-the-road, 27%; versus 53.0%, 35.3%, and 11.7% respectively for the total sample here. The sample under study here is slightly more conservative. The Campus I sample is very close, allowing for the difference in question wording, with 59.3%, 20.4%, and 20.4% respectively.

Support for Actions of Dissent

The level of student support for actions of dissent will be outlined here. Three aspects of support are being examined: having participated in certain dissent actions, accepting the participation of others in certain dissent actions, and willingness to possibly participate in such actions in the future. The relative sizes of the dissent groups, reference group, and the potential dissent group for various dissent activities will be compared.

In assessing attitudes of acceptance of others' participation in certain dissent actions, the approach in measuring attitudes suggested by Sherif et al. (1965: 19-26) was adopted. They suggest that an individual's stand toward an issue be assessed by procedures that yield the limits of the positions he accepts (latitude of acceptance) and the limits of the positions he rejects (latitude of rejection), relative to the bounds of available alternatives defined by the extreme positions on the issue. The procedure they outline is to present the individual with alternatives with respect to an issue, ranging from positive extreme to negative extreme. The individual is then asked to indicate the one alternative he most rejects and the one he most accepts, other alternatives he accepts and other alternatives he rejects. Four decisions are then obtained:

(1) Most accepted alternative.

(2) Most rejected alternative.

(3) Latitude or region of accepted alternatives.

(4) Latitudes or region of rejected alternatives.

Talking to others on a position was the most accepted action by respondents on all campuses. Approximately three-quarters of all respondents endorsed this action. Another 20% generally chose signing a petition as the most acceptable action, with a sprinkling of respondents choosing the other alternatives. There were no significant differences among the campuses. Clearly, the mildest form of protest is endorsed by the vast majority.

On the other hand, it is clear that burning record files is the most rejected with more than 80% choosing this action as the most rejected.

Civil disobedience, however, is chosen by 17.1 as the most rejected action. Apparently outright denial of law is more objectionable to some than is destruction of property.

The responses on both counts cluster at the ends of the distribution. Though all respondents are not unanimous, there is widespread agreement. This presents quite a different situation from one where people could differ considerably on what the most acceptable means of protest would be or where they endorsed the more vociferous means as the most acceptable. Under such circumstances, stress in the political system could bring instant crisis.

Now the discussion turns to the regions of acceptance and rejection of actions of dissent, the former being the obverse of the latter. For all campuses they appear in Table 11. For the acceptance table, the percentage for each item indicates the percentage of respondents who accepted that item and those below it. For the rejection table the percentage for each item indicates the percentage of respondents who rejected that item and those above it. They do not correspond exactly because of some dropoff in responding to one or the other directions.

From the total sample we see that the largest single group, about 40%, were willing to accept sitting-in and thus picketing, signing a petition, and talking to others to gain support for a position, but were not willing to accept engaging in civil disobedience such as taking a building or the burning of record files. Approximately 23% stopped with those actions generally recognized under law in the United States, namely, picketing, signing a petition, and talking, while about 24% were not willing to go this far but would only accept petition signing and talking as legitimate dissent activities. Only 2% would stop with talking, with 1% of the total rejecting even this action. On the other end, about 8% were willing to accept civil disobedience such as building takeovers, with another 1.7% willing to also accept burning record files.

Acceptance or rejection of actions of protest is apparently not linked to prescriptions of law for large numbers of the student respondents. This is true for both sides of the line with a relatively large group going beyond that which is generally considered lawful, and another relatively large group stopping short of acts considered lawful in their endorsement. With such a span of disagreement among student clients, it is a small wonder that protests of all types have generally sparked controversy in this country. In addition, organizational decision-makers must take this diversity of orientation into consideration in their decision-making.

There are some differences among campuses. Consistent with previously presented data, more Campus I respondents are willing to go further with acceptance of dissent actions than were those from the other campuses.

TABLE 11

Regions of Acceptance and Rejection of Actions of Dissent

	Talk to Others	Sign Petitions	Picket	Sit-In	Civil Disobedience	Burn Files	Number of Respondents	
Acceptance								
Campus I	0.0	11.4	20.3	46.8	16.5	5.1	158	(100.0)
Campus II	1.2	25.7	24.5	41.0	6.7	0.9	321	(100.0)
Campus III	2.4	22.4	24.9	42.4	6.8	1.0	205	(100.0)
Campus IV	4.1	27.7	24.1	37.9	4.1	2.1	195	(100.0)
Campus V	2.3	30.6	23.1	35.3	8.1	0.6	173	(100.0)
Total	2.0	24.1	23.6	40.6	7.9	1.7	1058	(100.0)
Rejection								
Campus I	0.0	0.7	15.1	20.4	46.7	17.1	158	(100.0)
Campus II	.3	1.5	26.2	24.9	40.9	6.2	321	(100.0)
Campus III	2.5	2.5	22.9	23.9	42.3	6.0	205	(100.0)
Campus IV	1.1	2.6	19.6	16.9	47.6	12.2	195	(100.0)
Campus V	1.8	3.6	32.5	21.3	33.1	7.7	173	(100.0)
Total	1.1	2.1	23.7	22.0	42.0	9.1	1058	(100.0)

Thus, 16.5% of the Campus I respondents—twice as many as the next highest campus—were willing to endorse the legitimacy of civil disobedience, while about 5% of the Campus I respondents were willing to accept the burning of record files by those protesting their grievances. Campus V respondents, on the other hand, are the most limiting of the campus respondents with 32.5% rejecting everything except petition signing and talking versus 23.7% for the sample as a whole.

With between approximately 44 to 48 % on each campus willing to accept the legitimacy of actions of dissent that go beyond those supported by law—that is, talking, petitioning, protesting—we see that a substantial reference group for relatively strong actions of dissent exists. Widespread support for talking on positions, signing petitions, picketing, and sitting-in can be found on any of the campuses under examination. Relatively small, but still significant support was found for civil disobedience, such as taking a building; while burning record files was largely rejected. With such a distribution of support, potential protest groups are able to select from a variety of measures of dissent action, some quite strong, and can be assured of considerable acceptance among their fellow students.

Thus, while there is considerable agreement on those measures most acceptable, there is a diversity of opinion with regard to how far clients will be willing to let their cohorts go in protest. Under such circumstances in particular cases, protestors may find vigorous supporters as well as vigorous opponents and neutrals of varying descriptions among the client group. Diversity will thus characterize most stress situations.

Next, the number of those indicating actual participation in each of the actions of dissent under examination will be presented. Respondents were asked if they had ever done any of the actions. The results appear in Table 12. The items are arranged from least to most frequent.

In terms of actual participation in actions of dissent, overall participation in the more active forms was not large for any of the campuses examined. Even on Campus I, only 19% had ever committed an act they considered to be in the realm of civil disobedience. The milder forms of dissent, talking and petition signing, account for the bulk of the activity. These items form a Guttman scale in the order presented with a coefficient of reproducibility of .94 and a coefficient of scalability of .64. Both measures are above those levels considered acceptable.

In comparing these results with the Harris national sample (1971), the respondents here were slightly less active than the nationwide student sample. For the national sample, participation for three acts was: 87% had signed a petition; 29% had picketed; and 18% had engaged in civil disobedience; versus 61.1%, 8.3%, and 8.7% respectively for the total sample here. Campus I is close to the national with 73.2%, 18.3%, and 19.0%

TABLE 12

Percentages of Respondents Having Participated in Actions of Dissent

	Destroyed Property		Sat-in *		Picketed *		Civil Disobedience *		Talked on Position *		Signed Petition *	
	yes	no	yes	no	yes	no	yes	no	yes	no	yes	no
Campus I	7 (4.2)	161 (95.8)	17 (10.3)	148 (89.7)	30 (18.3)	134 (81.7)	32 (19.0)	136 (81.0)	96 (58.5)	68 (41.5)	120 (73.2)	44 (26.8)
Campus II	4 (1.2)	328 (98.8)	12 (3.6)	318 (96.4)	24 (7.3)	305 (92.7)	16 (4.8)	317 (95.2)	112 (33.8)	219 (66.2)	225 (68.4)	104 (31.6)
Campus III	3 (1.4)	209 (98.6)	4 (1.9)	208 (98.1)	10 (4.8)	199 (95.2)	11 (5.2)	201 (94.8)	62 (29.7)	147 (70.3)	122 (58.9)	85 (41.1)
Campus IV	3 (1.5)	199 (98.8)	15 (6.9)	188 (93.1)	19 (8.9)	184 (91.1)	17 (8.5)	184 (91.5)	41 (20.3)	161 (79.7)	94 (46.8)	107 (53.2)
Campus V	7 (3.9)	172 (96.1)	7 (3.9)	172 (96.1)	8 (4.5)	171 (95.5)	19 (10.6)	160 (89.4)	52 (29.1)	127 (70.9)	99 (55.3)	80 (44.7)
Total	24 (2.2)	1069 (97.8)	54 (5.0)	1038 (95.0)	91 (8.3)	993 (91.7)	95 (8.7)	998 (91.3)	363 (33.5)	722 (66.5)	660 (61.1)	420 (38.9)

*Chi-square difference significant at .01 level.

respectively. These six items examined above will be used as a scale to test the hypotheses.

Also of interest are the numbers of respondents who indicated they would participate in the protest activities. They were asked if they would ever participate in the same actions presented above. The results appear in Table 13. Again, the items are arranged from least to most frequent. The increase for most of the items over the participation item is substantial. Whereas, 8.3% of the total respondents reported that they had engaged in picketing, 46.3% indicated they would be willing to do so; and whereas 5.0% of the total respondents reported they had participated in a sit-in, 38.6% indicated a willingness to do so. Undoubtedly, these responses to the question "would you ever" represent a willingness to engage in the indicated action if provoked enough. The only action not registering a sizable gain over the percentage that have actually done the act was destroying property. Campus I respondents registered a gain from 4.2 to 19.5%, but the other campus increases were on the order of 3%. Apparently, there are deep-seated attitudinal prohibitions against the destruction of property for purposes of protest. This contrasts with the percentages willing to sign petitions of 88.2% and talking on positions of 82.8%. Whereas the actual participants for most actions were but a small minority, the potential participant group for four of the six actions is either a large minority or a substantial majority. The range even here is quite striking from what the individuals considered strong to milder forms of protest. Whereas 88.2% would sign a petition, less than half this proportion (38.6) would be willing to participate in a sit-in. Willingness to participate drops off as the form of protest becomes stronger.

In terms of potential participation for actions of dissent, even the stronger forms receive considerable willingness to participate. The items form a Guttman scale in the order presented with a coefficient of reproducibility of .94 and a coefficient of scalability of .77. Both measures are above those levels considered acceptable. The above six items will also be used as a scale to test the hypotheses.

Again making the comparison with the Harris sample, the total sample here shows somewhat less willingness to participate. For the Harris sample, participation in the three acts was sign a petition, 96%; picket, 60%; and engage in civil disobedience, 40%; versus 88.2%, 46.3%, and 21.6% respectively for the total sample here. Campus I respondents again are close to the national picture with 90.3%, 60.7%, and 38.5% respectively for the three acts.

Summing up, support for actions of dissent is varied according to level of personal involvement. Respondents were more willing to accept the legitimacy of others participating in the various actions, than were they

TABLE 13

Percentages of Respondents Willing to Participate in Actions of Dissent

	Destroy Property*		Civil Disobedience*		Sit-in*		Picket*		Talk on Position*		Sign Petition**	
	yes	no	yes	no	yes	no	yes	no	yes	no	yes	no
Campus I	37 (19.5)	136 (80.5)	65 (38.5)	104 (61.5)	88 (51.8)	82 (48.2)	102 (60.7)	66 (39.3)	147 (91.3)	14 (8.7)	149 (90.3)	16 (9.7)
Campus II	16 (4.8)	318 (95.2)	64 (19.2)	269 (80.8)	125 (37.5)	208 (62.5)	157 (47.9)	177 (53.0)	269 (83.5)	53 (16.5)	311 (93.4)	22 (6.6)
Campus III	9 (4.2)	202 (95.3)	39 (18.2)	172 (81.5)	71 (33.6)	140 (66.4)	97 (45.8)	115 (54.2)	170 (81.3)	39 (18.7)	184 (86.8)	28 (13.2)
Campus IV	9 (4.5)	190 (95.5)	36 (17.9)	165 (82.1)	75 (37.1)	127 (62.9)	84 (42.0)	116 (58.0)	162 (80.2)	40 (19.8)	167 (83.5)	33 (16.5)
Campus V	12 (6.7)	167 (93.3)	32 (17.9)	147 (82.1)	63 (35.6)	114 (64.4)	66 (36.9)	113 (63.1)	140 (78.2)	39 (21.8)	150 (83.8)	29 (16.2)
Total	79 (7.2)	1013 (92.7)	236 (21.6)	857 (78.4)	422 (38.6)	671 (61.4)	506 (46.3)	587 (53.7)	888 (82.8)	185 (17.2)	961 (88.2)	129 (11.8)

*Chi-square difference significant at .01 level.
**Chi-square difference significant at .05 level.

willing to either participate themselves or own up to having participated, in such activities in the past. They were also more inclined to express their willingness to participate at some future point than to have already participated. On all three measures, the percentage of respondents supporting actions declined as the form of the protest increased in strength.

Organizational authorities can expect that protest groups engaging in the milder forms of protest may be quite large, while those engaging in the stronger forms may be substantially smaller. This finding coincides with previous occurrences. However, it may be useful to know that clients come to specific situations with such built-in predispositions.

In examining the three measures of support for actions of dissent, two patterns emerge. The first is that as the forms of protest get stronger support falls off. Second, as incidence of endorsement for all actions of dissent increases (though not at the same rate), the respondents personal involvement in the act lessens. In short, protest groups are much more likely to obtain endorsement from other students than to get them to join in their actions.

Organizational authorities may expect that as the ferocity of the protest acts increase, the participant, potential participant, and reference groups will decrease in size. Such a condition aids organizational maintenance during periods of stress.

HYPOTHESIS TESTING

The basic models to be tested were presented earlier. Here, the hypotheses will be tested first, and the models second. The procedures followed to operationalize the variables for the purpose of inclusion in the testing procedure will first be outlined.

First, the background characteristics—permissiveness, father's education, mother's education, income, and grade point average—are all treated as previously operationalized. Major in college is dichotomized with behavioral sciences, humanities, and fine arts in one category; and business, education, sciences, and all others in the second category.

Secondly, in regard to attitudinal characteristics, ideology is dichotomized into liberal and conservative categories. For each individual respondent a standardized factor score on each of the five factors of attitudes toward authorities and the two factors of radical regime change were computed. These scores will be used to operationalize the authority variables. The factor scores represent the individual respondent's score on each of the factors derived and hence represent the degree of his acceptance of the legitimacy of authority for each type of authority. These scores can then be correlated with other variables for purposes of hypothesis and model testing. In other words, instead of using the 24 individual items for measuring the legitimacy of authorities, the factor scores for the general, bureaucratic, organizational, police, and city authority dimensions are used for each individual. Likewise, instead of using the eight items measuring radical regime change, the factor scores on the institutional regime authority and process regime authority dimensions are used.

As mentioned previously, the three dissent support variables utilized are acceptance of others participation, having participated, and willingness to participate in various actions of dissent. Acceptance is measured by the individual scores according to his region of acceptance covering the six actions—talking on a position, signing a petition, picketing, sitting-in, engaging in civil disobedience, and burning record files. For example, an individual accepting talking, petitioning, and picketing, but rejecting sitting-in, engaging in civil disobedience and burning record files would have a score of three. Possible scores then range from zero to six. Figure 5 illustrates the rejection regions and possible scores.

Several items thought to be indicators of a student's participation or willingness to participate in various actions of dissent were tested for scalability. The frequencies for the items were presented previously.

The three scales referring to the three types of support for actions of dissent will be termed: acceptance, have participated, and would participate. In both the correlation and regression analyses that follow, pairwise

Burning Files	Civil Disobedience	Sit-in	Picket	Petition	Talking	Score
X	X	X	X	X	X	6
	X	X	X	X	X	5
		X	X	X	X	4
			X	X	X	3
				X	X	2
					X	1
						0

Figure 5: Rejection Regions of Acceptance of Dissent Actions

deletion was used for missing data. Under pairwise deletion, a case is omitted from the computation of a given simple coefficient if the value of either of the two variables is missing. A case is included in the computation of all simple coefficients for which it has complete data.

Relationship Between Background and Attitudinal Characteristics

The first set of hypotheses specify the relationship between particular background characteristics and the attitudinal components under examination in this paper. The underlying supposition is that certain family and educational socialization experiences lead to certain attitudes dealing with authority and ideology. These hypotheses are found in Figure 6.

Table 14 presents the intercorrelations of these socialization background characteristics with the attitudes toward authorities, radical regime change attitudes, and ideology in simple and partial form for the total sample.

As can be seen, the background socialization characteristics generally show little impact on attitudes toward authorities. For the total sample, these six socialization variables together account for from .5% to 1.5% of the variance on the five dimensions of attitudes toward authorities. Also, for all five of the individual campuses, 20 of the 25 total possible multiple correlations show under 5% of the variance explained. Thus, even though there are some statistically significant confirmations of hypotheses tested, these socialization variables are not very helpful in explaining much of the variance in client attitudes toward authorities.

It must be concluded then that family socialization background characteristics show little connection with respondent acceptance or rejection of the legitimacy of political system authorities.

With respect to educational socialization, hypotheses 4a and 5a predict that those with behavioral science and humanities majors and with higher grade point averages would tend to reject the legitimacy of position authority. Major shows no significant relationship in the total sample. Within campuses for major only the simple and partial correlations on bureaucratic authority at one campus and the sample for organizational authority at another are significant. In regard to grade point average, small correlations in the total sample for police and city authority are significant at the .05 level but in the direction opposite of that predicted (that is, those with lower grade point averages tend to reject these types of authority more, but the relationship is extremely slight). Within campuses the simple and partial correlations for police authority are significant at .05 but generally account for less than 2% of the variance and for city authority only

H₁a. Those who come from homes where their parents stressed a lower degree of obedience will reject the legitimacy of authorities to a higher degree than those who come from homes where their parents stressed a higher degree of obedience.

Low
Obedience

+ → General Authority Rejection
+ → Bureaucratic Authority Rejection
+ → University Authority Rejection
+ → Police Authority Rejection
+ → City Authority Rejection

H₁b. Those who come from homes where their parents stressed a lower degree of obedience will more strongly want a radical change in regime than those who come from homes where their parents stressed a higher degree of obedience.

Low
Obedience ————— + ————→ Institutional Regime Change

Low
Obedience ————— + ————→ Process Regime Change

H₆ Those who come from homes where their parents stressed a lower degree of obedience will consider themselves liberal while those who come from homes where their parents stressed a higher degree of obedience will consider themselves conservative.

Low
Obedience ————— + ————→ Ideological Liberalism

H₂a. Those whose parents have a higher degree of education will reject the legitimacy of authorities to a higher degree than those whose parents have a lower degree of education.

Father's
Education ——— +
Mother's
Education ——— +

+ → General Authority Rejection
+ → Bureaucratic Authority Rejection
+ → University Authority Rejection
+ → Police Authority Rejection
+ → City Authority Rejection

Figure 6: Socialization—Attitudinal Hypotheses

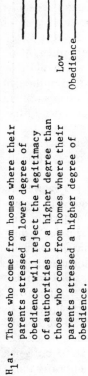

Figure 6 (Continued)

H₄b. Those who have higher grade point averages will more strongly want a radical change in regime than those who have lower grade point averages.

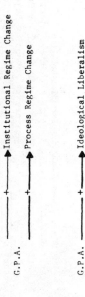

G.P.A. —————— + ——————▶ Institutional Regime Change

+ ——————▶ Process Regime Change

H₉. Those who have higher grade point averages will consider themselves liberal while those who have lower grade point averages will consider themselves conservative.

G.P.A. —————— + ——————▶ Ideological Liberalism

H₅a. Those majoring in the social sciences and humanities will reject the legitimacy of authorities to a higher degree than those who have majors in business, the sciences, and education.

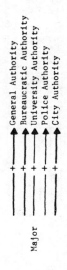

Major —————— + ——————▶ General Authority

+ ——————▶ Bureaucratic Authority

+ ——————▶ University Authority

+ ——————▶ Police Authority

+ ——————▶ City Authority

H₅b. Those majoring in the social sciences and humanities will more strongly want a radical change in regime than those majoring in business, the sciences, and education.

Major —————— + ——————▶ Institutional Regime Authority

+ ——————▶ Process Regime Change

H₁₀. Those majoring in the social sciences and humanities will consider themselves liberal while those in business, the sciences, and education will consider themselves conservative.

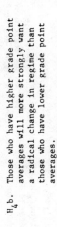

Major —————— + ——————▶ Ideological Liberalism

Figure 6 (Continued)

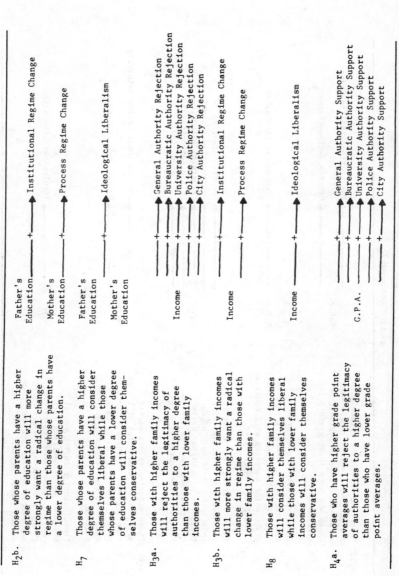

H₂b. Those whose parents have a higher degree of education will more strongly want a radical change in regime than those whose parents have a lower degree of education.

Father's Education ────── + ──────▶ Institutional Regime Change

Mother's Education ────── + ──────▶ Process Regime Change

H₇ Those whose parents have a higher degree of education will consider themselves liberal while those whose parents have a lower degree of education will consider themselves conservative.

Father's Education ────── + ──────▶ Ideological Liberalism

Mother's Education

H₃a. Those with higher family incomes will reject the legitimacy of authorities to a higher degree than those with lower family incomes.

Income
+ ──▶ General Authority Rejection
+ ──▶ Bureaucratic Authority Rejection
+ ──▶ University Authority Rejection
+ ──▶ Police Authority Rejection
+ ──▶ City Authority Rejection

H₃b. Those with higher family incomes will more strongly want a radical change in regime than those with lower family incomes.

Income
+ ──▶ Institutional Regime Change
+ ──▶ Process Regime Change

H₈ Those with higher family incomes will consider themselves liberal while those with lower family incomes will consider themselves conservative.

Income ────── + ──────▶ Ideological Liberalism

H₄a. Those who have higher grade point averages will reject the legitimacy of authorities to a higher degree than those who have lower grade point averages.

G.P.A.
+ ──▶ General Authority Support
+ ──▶ Bureaucratic Authority Support
+ ──▶ University Authority Support
+ ──▶ Police Authority Support
+ ──▶ City Authority Support

TABLE 14

**Multiple and Partial Correlations of Background Characteristics
with Attitudinal Characteristics—Total Sample**

	Obedience	Father's Education	Mother's Education	Income	Major	GPA	R^2
Attitudinal Characteristics							
ATTITUDES TOWARD AUTHORITIES							
General	.024	−.008	.024	−.040	.033	−.030	.005
Bureaucratic	.051*	.030	−.046	.016	.045	−.030	.008
University	.090**	.055*	−.056*	.040	.028	.006	.015
Police	.054*	.049	−.022	.005	.015	−.068*	.010
City	.012	−.061*	.015	.007	−.002	−.055*	.007
RADICAL REGIME CHANGE							
Institutional	.087**	.042	.019	−.026	.060*	−.109**	.029
Process	−.046	−.035	.028	−.023	.064*	−.153**	.035
IDEOLOGY							
Conservatism– Liberalism	.106**	−.005	.037	−.022	.059*	−.030	.019

*Significant at .05 level.
**Significant at .01 level.

at Campus I are the correlations significant at .05. Generally then, college educational experience has little effect on attitudes toward political system authorities.

Hypotheses 1b, 2b, 3b, 4b, and 5b deal with the relationship between these six socialization characteristics and attitudes toward radical change of regime, both institutional and process. These six background variables account for only 2.9% of the variance in institutional regime change attitudes and 3.5% for process regime change attitudes for the total sample.

Permissiveness seems also to have little effect on propensity toward radical regime change attitudes with the correlation reaching significance at one campus which was enough to push the total sample to slight significance.

Academic major is significant for institutional change attitudes at the .01 level for the total sample, but only the simple correlation at Campus II is significant for within campus correlations. For process change, small significant correlations were found for the total Campus I and Campus III samples. The relationships between grade point average and both institutional and process change for Campus II and Campus III are significant for both simple and partial correlations at the .01 level but in the opposite direction from that predicted. Process alone was significant at .05 in Campus V. All correlations are slight and explain little of the variance.

In sum, with a few slight scattered exceptions, the overall conclusion reached is that these family and educational socialization variables help very little in predicting attitude toward radical change of regime.

Hypotheses 6, 7, 8, 9, and 10 predict the relationships between the six socialization characteristics and ideology. All six variables account for only 1.9% of the variance in the total sample. Obedience is significant at Campus II at .05 and Campus III at .05 and thus for the total sample at .01. Parents' education and income have no significant effect on the ideology of the respondents. The partial correlations for major are signficant at .05 for the total sample due to the large sample size but fail to reach significance for a single campus. Grade point average has significant correlations (at Campus II only) but in the direction opposite to that predicted. It must be concluded, then, that these socialization characteristics seem to have almost no effect on ideological attitude of the respondents examined.

In summary, neither the family socialization characteristics—stress on obedience, parent's education, and income—nor education socialization characteristics—academic major and grade point average—have a significant effect on the attitudinal variables under consideration. The hypotheses predicting relationships between these background socialization variables and authority and ideological attitudes are not confirmed.

These findings suggest that those explanations for challenge to the authority that rest solely or primarily on emphasizing the direct role of the American middle or upper-middle-class family need to be substantially modified. Apparently, other crucial factors need to be taken into consideration. In the final section the discussion will suggest some of these.

Secondly, explanations that rest on academic characteristics of students for their political behavior also require modifications. Alternative approaches in this respect will be discussed in the final section.

Relationship Between Background Characteristics and Support for Actions of Dissent

Another set of hypotheses suggest possible relationships between the background characteristics and support for actions of dissent as specified above. Some researchers cited earlier postulated that these socialization characteristics were more often found among campus activists. These researchers were dealing with groups participating in particular protest events. In the current study the hypotheses will be tested upon a broad sample of students. These socialization experiences may possibly have a direct effect on the propensity to support actions of dissent independent of authority or ideological attitudes.

To test the relationship between family and educational socialization characteristics and support for actions of dissent, the hypotheses in Figure 7 will be tested.

From Table 15 the relationship between the background socialization variables and support for actions of dissent is not much stronger than was the relationship between these background socialization variables and the attitudinal variables. In general, they do not account for a large amount of the variance in the behavioral dependent variables. (For the total sample these six socialization variables explain 2.8% of the variance in the respondents' acceptance of others' participation in various protest acts, 3.3% of the variance in having themselves participated, and 4.1% of the variance in willingness to participate in such actions. For a given individual campus the maximum amount of variance explained was 2.7% for acceptance, 8.8% for having participated, and 7.6% for willingness to participate—all at Campus III.)

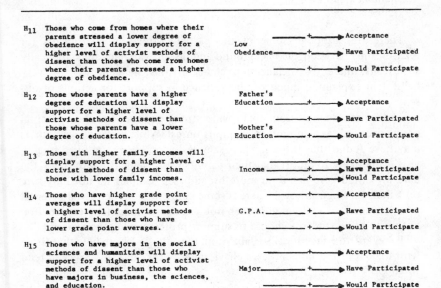

H_{11} Those who come from homes where their parents stressed a lower degree of obedience will display support for a higher level of activist methods of dissent than those who come from homes where their parents stressed a higher degree of obedience.

H_{12} Those whose parents have a higher degree of education will display support for a higher level of activist methods of dissent than those whose parents have a lower degree of education.

H_{13} Those with higher family incomes will display support for a higher level of activist methods of dissent than those with lower family incomes.

H_{14} Those who have higher grade point averages will display support for a higher level of dissent than those who have lower grade point averages.

H_{15} Those who have majors in the social sciences and humanities will display support for a higher level of activist methods of dissent than those who have majors in business, the sciences, and education.

Figure 7: Socialization—Behavioral Hypotheses

TABLE 15
Multiple and Partial Correlations of Background Characteristics with Support for Actions of Dissent

Support for Actions of Dissent	Obedience	Father's Education	Mother's Education	Income	Major	G.P.A.	R^2
Total Sample							
Acceptance	.104**	.066*	.027	-.029	.078**	-.003	.028
Have Participated	.108**	.072*	.041	.033	.018	.022	.033
Would Participate	.145**	.066*	.026	.031	.061*	.022	.041
Campus I Sample							
Acceptance	.056	-.010	-.048	-.076	.110	.095	.033
Have Participated	-.013	.111	-.144*	.028	.108	.052	.037
Would Participate	.061	.065	-.046	-.052	.022	.089	.018
Campus II Sample							
Acceptance	.189**	.086	-.038	.065	.023	.023	.055
Have Participated	.087	.023	.072	.016	-.056	-.032	.021
Would Participate	.145**	.091	-.011	.031	.049	.002	.040
Campus III Sample							
Acceptance	.068	-.065	.135*	.029	.126*	-.055	.052
Have Participated	.032	.026	.084	.114	.027	-.011	.023
Would Participate	.096	-.032	.114	.135*	.062	-.066	.030
Campus IV Sample							
Acceptance	.044	.083	-.003	-.146*	.020	.019	.027
Have Participated	.258**	.111	.049	-.054	-.002	.061	.088
Would Participate	.261**	.087	-.054	-.038	.028	.098	.076
Campus V Sample							
Acceptance	.069	.034	.000	.029	.148*	-.105	.041
Have Participated	.091	.016	-.037	.114	-.008	.044	.024
Would Participate	.100	.049	.062	.135*	.114	-.007	.075

*Significant at .05 level.
**Significant at .01 level.

Therefore, although some of the partial correlation coefficients for relationships between the background and dissent variables are statistically significant, these six socialization characteristics are generally not very helpful in explaining much of the variance in support for actions of dissent.

These data do not seem to provide strong support for the "parental permissiveness" explanation for campus unrest. While previous researchers may have found that those in their samples, which were confined to activists, were likely to report that their parents were "lenient" with them, the data presented here based on more broad-based samples do not fully support their findings, although there is some confirmation. Perceived parental permissiveness in childrearing does not provide a consistent explanation as to why some students choose to support protest while others do not.

In regard to educational socialization, hypothesis 12 predicts that those with majors in the humanities, behavioral sciences, and fine arts will tend to support stronger forms of protest action than will those majoring in business, education, or the sciences. Hypothesis 13 predicts more support for protest actions will come from those with higher grade point averages. The previous studies of activist background reviewed previously revealed that the activists interviewed were drawn disproportionately from the humanities and social sciences. Further, Keniston argued they tend to be the more intelligent students.

However, little support is found in these data for a relationship between educational socialization experience and support for actions of dissent.

In general, neither the family socialization characteristics—stress on obedience, parents' education, income, nor the educational socialization characteristics—academic major and grade point average have a substantial effect in determining support for actions of dissent. This was true for all three forms of support—acceptance of other students participating in stronger forms of protest actions, participating themselves, or saying that they would participate. For the most part, then, the hypotheses predicting relationships between these background socialization variables and support for actions of dissent are not confirmed.

Previous research that has heavily stressed the permissiveness of the family and parental and family socioeconomic characteristics in explaining campus activism would seem to find little support from these data. Perhaps the earlier studies in concentrating on those participating in demonstrations alone attributed more importance to these characteristics then they deserve. More broad-based samples indicate that other students with similar backgrounds do not choose to participate in activist methods. Socioeconomic class by itself then does not seem to provide much of an explanation for campus activism. Also, Clarke and Egan (1972) and also Dunlap (1970) report similar findings. Dunlap observed that growing involvement in activism necessarily involves broader-based recruitment.

Relationship Between Attitudinal Characteristics and Support for Actions of Dissent

The final set of hypotheses stated have to do with the relationship between three types of attitudinal variables and support for various actions of dissent. The attitudinal variables include:

(1) the dimensions of attitudes toward authorities,

(2) the dimensions of attitudes toward radical regime change, and

(3) ideological attitudes.

The first component is concerned with the individual's acceptance of the legitimacy of the authority of organizational and political system authorities. The second is concerned with the individual's acceptance of the legitimacy of the authority of the regime. The third attitudinal component is concerned with the individual's evaluation and approach to system politics and issues. The underlying supposition here is that if the individual possesses certain attitudinal characteristics in these areas it is likely that they will carry over into behavioral areas concerned with compliance/noncompliance in terms of protest. The relevant hypothesis appear in Figure 8.

Tables 16 and 17 present the simple and partial intercorrelations of the attitudinal variables of dimensions of attitudes toward authorities, radical regime change attitudes, and ideological attitudes with the three support for actions of dissent variables for the total sample and for each campus sample.

It can be seen from Table 17 that taken together the attitudinal variables have a fairly strong impact on support for actions of dissent. For the total sample the eight attitudinal variables explain 21.8% of the variance with respect to acceptance of participation in various actions of dissent, and 25.1% of the variance in expressed willingness to engage in various methods of dissent. For Campus I alone, the percentages of explained variance is even higher than for the total sample with 42.5% for acceptance, 35.1% for having participated, and 34.7% for willingness to participate in various actions of dissent. The attitudinal variables collectively help explain variation in support for various protest actions.

Turning to the individual simple correlations in Table 16 for the total sample, every attitudinal variable with the exception of the city authority factor is significantly correlated with at least two or the measures of support for actions of dissent. Of the seven remaining attitudinal measures, only the correlations of general authority with acceptance and process regime change attitude with having participated in dissent are not significantly correlated. Thus, 16 of the 19 significant correlations attain significance at the .01 level. However, when partialed, several of the correlations drop below significance.

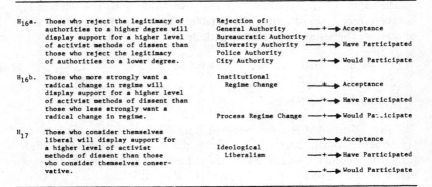

Figure 8: Attitudinal—Behavioral Hypotheses

TABLE 16

Simple Correlations of Attitudinal Characteristics with Support for Actions of Dissent

Support for Actions of Dissent	General Authority	Bureau-cratic Authority	University Authority	Police Authority	City Authority	Institu-tional Regime	Process Regime	Conserva-tism Liberalism
Total Sample								
Acceptance	.045	.071*	.143**	.086**	.019	.384**	.066*	.373**
Have Participated	.077**	.078**	.217**	.082**	.044	.290**	.044	.317**
Would Participate	.080**	.079**	.176**	.127**	.011	.379**	.065*	.411**
Campus I Sample								
Acceptance	.125	.149*	.332**	.176*	-.031	.477**	.171*	.478**
Have Participated	.224**	.114	.342**	.158*	.034	.435**	.095	.397**
Would Participate	.200**	.080	.299**	.172*	.031	.406**	.081	.428**
Campus II Sample								
Acceptance	.035	.132**	.052	.060	.006	.385**	.032	.334**
Have Participated	.049	.134**	.165**	.076	.056	.259**	.090	.330**
Would Participate	.052	.140**	.156**	.126**	.065	.418**	.122*	.390**
Campus III Sample								
Acceptance	.031	.044	-.004	.048	.072	.282**	.043*	.346**
Have Participated	-.009	-.021	.146*	.030	.035	.112	.016	.104**
Would Participate	-.046	.046	.095	.126*	-.061	.292**	.041	.338**
Campus IV Sample								
Acceptance	-.091	.010	.222**	.135*	.043	.304**	-.036	.294**
Have Participated	.138*	.026	.196*	.088	.036	.252**	.060	.350**
Would Participate	.043	.081	.156*	.162*	-.022	.374**	-.008	.454**
Campus V Sample								
Acceptance	.092	-.058	.104	-.035	-.019	.390**	.109	.412**
Have Participated	.017	.048	.175**	-.032	-.008	.265**	.038	.317**
Would Participate	.094	-.024	.107	-.034	-.026	.304**	.097	.409**

*Significant at .05 level.
**Significant at .01 level.

TABLE 17

Multiple and Partial Correlations of Attitudinal Characteristics
with Support for Actions of Dissent

Support for Actions of Dissent	General Authority	Bureaucratic Authority	Organizational Authority	Police Authority	City Authority	Institutional Regime	Process Regime	Conservatism Liberalism	R^2
Total Sample									
Acceptance	.006	-.013	.092**	.044	.001	.264**	.050	.262**	.218
Have Participated	.057*	.019	.188**	.056*	.036	.156**	.013	.231**	.171
Would Participate	.050	-.004	.134**	.095**	-.007	.235**	.038	.309**	.251
Campus I Sample									
Acceptance	.030	-.068	.239**	.179*	-.098	.243**	.181*	.428**	.425
Have Participated	.194*	-.070	.257**	.144	.017	.187*	.019	.348**	.351
Would Participate	.172*	-.111	.230**	.181*	.011	.149	.007	.400**	.347
Campus II Sample									
Acceptance	.023	.041	.003	-.030	-.010	.272**	.041	.195**	.187
Have Participated	-.063	.066	.136*	.063	.054	.123*	.065	.234**	.160
Would Participate	.041	.037	.115*	.109*	.049	.292**	.124*	.241**	.268
Campus III Sample									
Acceptance	-.029	-.002	-.038	-.006	.045	.159*	.114	.276**	.162
Have Participated	-.021	-.047	.139*	.008	.019	.065	.005	.073	.038
Would Participate	-.086	-.012	.071	.088	-.105	.190**	.026	.258**	.173
Campus IV Sample									
Acceptance	-.112	-.040	.201**	.035	.030	.235*	-.006	.208**	.191
Have Participated	.139*	-.056	.184**	-.024	.031	.165*	.048	.287**	.196
Would Participate	.022	-.004	.143*	.013	-.027	.264**	-.009	.366**	.283
Campus V Sample									
Acceptance	.031	-.082	.059	.003	-.019	.286**	.042	.321**	.255
Have Participated	-.234	.082	.184*	-.001	.012	.176*	-.098	.257**	.168
Would Participate	.049	-.026	.081	-.005	-.015	.178*	.043	.339**	.270

*Significant at .05 level.
**Significant at .01 level.

With respect to attitudes toward authority, partialing eliminates significance for bureaucratic authority, reduces one of the two correlations below significance for general authority and the other to the .05 level, and eliminates one and reduces another to .05 for police authority. Only organizational authority retains significant correlation at the .01 level with all three measures of support for actions of dissent for the total sample. The university organization is the closest subsystem to the individual students. This fact seems to have relevance for the relationship of student attitudes toward authority and dissent. Organizational authority may provide the link between the authority structure and compliance behavior.

For individual campuses the pattern is consistent, with correlations for all but organizational authority generally reduced under partialing. Organizational authority, however, has significant partial correlations for all campuses with at least one measure of support for actions of dissent. The relationship is strongest at Campus I. Hypothesis 16a is then partially confirmed.

In regard to regime change attitudes for the total sample, the two significant correlations for process regime change disappear when partialed, while the three correlations for institutional regime change remain significant at the .01 level. Within the campus samples, process regime change is largely not significant, while for institutional regime change only the correlation with willingness to participate at Campus I disappears under partialing, although a reduction in the magnitude of the correlations is observed for all campuses. Hypothesis 16b is then confirmed for institutional regime change.

Looking at ideological attitude, conservatism-liberalism correlates at the .01 level for both simple and partial correlations for all measures for the total sample and 14 of the 15 possible measures for the individual campuses. The partial correlations for Campus I are particularly strong explaining approximately 16, 10, and 16% of the variance for acceptance, having participated, and willingness to participate respectively. Hypothesis 17 is then confirmed.

In reference to the types of attitudes examined with relevance to support for actions of dissent, ideological or specific support attitudes would seem to be particularly strong while authority or diffuse support attitudes would be somewhat weaker but still significant.

RELATIVE PROPORTION OF VARIANCE EXPLAINED BY INDEPENDENT VARIABLES

The discussion now examines how the variables selected have done in predicting support for actions of dissent. Of course in behavioral research the expectation is that a set of variables will explain a portion of the variance in a dependent variable, not necessarily all or most of it. If this expectation is met, theoretical significance may be attached to the variables thus examined. Therefore, the discussion will examine the effect of the variables previously delineated.

Table 18 shows the relative proportions of variance explained by the various combinations of variables. It can be seen from column A that the background and attitudinal variables taken together do fairly well in esplaining a significant proportion of the variance in support for actions of dissent. For the total sample these variables account for 23.0% of the variance in accepting others' participation in various acts of protest, 19.2% in having participated in various protest acts oneself, and 27.3% in willingness to participate in acts of protest in the future. The individual campus results are similar to the total sample with the exception of Campus I, the large residential university, for which the 14 variables do even better explaining 44.9% in acceptance, 36.0% in having participated and 36.7% in willingness to participate. This may indicate a strengthening of the impact of these variables related to situational influences.

TABLE 18
Proportion of Variance in Support for Actions of Dissent Explained by Background and Attitudinal Characteristics

Support for Actions of Dissent	A. Explained by all 14 variables R^2	B. Explained by 6 background characteristics Only R^2	C. Explained by 8 attitudinal characteristics Only R^2	D. Explained by 3 attitudinal characteristics Only R^2
Total Sample				
Acceptance	.230	.028	.218	.214
Have Participated	.192	.033	.171	.164
Would Participate	.273	.041	.251	.240
Campus I				
Acceptance	.449	.033	.425	.368
Have Participated	.360	.037	.351	.298
Would Participate	.367	.018	.347	.287
Campus II				
Acceptance	.222	.055	.187	.183
Have Participated	.172	.021	.160	.142
Would Participate	.288	.040	.268	.240
Campus III				
Acceptance	.198	.052	.162	.149
Have Participated	.065	.023	.038	.035
Would Participate	.198	.030	.173	.151
Campus IV				
Acceptance	.240	.027	.191	.177
Have Participated	.274	.088	.196	.175
Would Participate	.333	.076	.283	.282
Campus V				
Acceptance	.279	.041	.255	.248
Have Participated	.193	.024	.168	.153
Would Participate	.255	.075	.210	.206

To determine the relative explanatory value of the background versus the attitudinal variables, column B shows the proportion of variance explained by the six background variables alone and column C shows the proportion explained by the eight attitudinal variables alone. By themselves the background variables explain relatively small proportions of the variance in measures of support for actions of dissent, while the attitudinal variables by themselves do considerably better. For the total sample the background variables explain 2.8, 3.3, and 4.1% of the variance, while the attitudinal variables explain 21.8, 17.1, and 25.1% of the variance in acceptance, having participated, and willingness to participate respectively. Within the campus samples the results are similar. The eight attitudinal variables do almost as well as the 14 variables together. At Campus I, for example, the difference in variance explained by the eight attitudinal variables by themselves and the full 14 variables is less than 3% for each of the three measures of protest support.

Head et al. (1972: 237, 79), in a nationwide study of the attitudes of American men toward violence, found that background factors added very little to the explanatory power of the psychological characteristics in explaining orientations toward violence for social change. They did find that how men felt about the legitimacy of the state affected how they defined acts as being violent.

Taking the analysis a step further, the three attitudinal variables that were most significant in predicting support for actions of dissent are presented. These were attitudes toward university authorities, institutional regime change attitude, and ideological attitude. The proportion of the variance explained in the dependent variables by these three variables is found in column D. These three variables do relatively as well in predicting support for actions of dissent as do the eight attitudinal variables combined. Generally, only very slight reductions in variance explained are involved. For the total sample the reductions are on the order of 1% or less. In sum, these three attitudinal variables do about as well as all eight attitudinal variables and all 14 variables combined in predicting support for actions of dissent. For this reason, these three variables will be utilized as the attitudinal variables in the testing of the theoretical models.

MODEL TESTING

Previously, four possible models were proposed to account for the relationships discussed. These were:

(1) the *developmental* model hypothesizing a relationships from background characteristics to the attitudinal characteristics to the support for actions of dissent;

(2) the *spurious* model hypothesizing no direct relationship between the attitudinal variables and support for actions of dissent but both being explained by the background characteristics;

(3) the *independence* model hypothesizing a relationship between the background characteristics and the measure of support for dissent, and also a relationship between the attitudinal characteristics and measures of support for dissent, but no relationship between the attitudinal and background characteristics; and

(4) the *hybrid* model hypothesizing a direct relationship of the background characteristics to support for actions of dissent and a developmental sequence through the attitudinal variables to support for actions of dissent.

In addition, one line of research was discussed previously that hypothesized that the developmental model would be most helpful in explaining the behavior under examination. This was that which suggested that socialization experiences had let to authority and ideological attitudes and then to behavior.

The next step is obviously to empirically test these theoretical models to arrive at the most supportable explanation. However, in selecting a methodology that would allow this to be done, conventional methods entail some difficulty.

Following the argument delineated by Cnudde and McCrone (1969) who previously addressed this problem, normally in a test of a developmental sequence such as the developmental model B $\rightarrow$ A $\rightarrow$ S discussed above, a control for the hypothesized intervening variable (A) would be made to determine whether the original relationship between the independent (B) and dependent (S) variable still remains. In making the test, an attempt is made to choose between the developmental sequence model and another model in which the test variable does not intervene and effects from the independent variable remain. However, when testing for spuriousness by using a control such as the spurious model

discussed above, normally a partial for the independent variable (B) would be made which supposedly accounts for any relationship between (A) and (S) in this model. If the correlation between the two hypothesized variables does not disappear, presumably this model is incorrect.

In both of the above described tests, an attempt is made to choose between the hypothesized model and a second model. However, in the present case the attempt is made to choose between models associated with the two tests: developmental sequence and spuriousness models. The conventional testing procedures are inadequate. For a full explanation of the problem, see Cnudde and McCrone (1969).

The procedure followed here is to control using unstandardized regression coefficients rather than partial correlation. The partial regression coefficients are utilized with controls for both spuriousness and developmental sequences to determine if the spurious, developmental, hybrid, or independence model is the most appropriate.

If a test of spuriousness on significant zero-order regression coefficients does not yield a reduction in the regression of acceptance of protest methods on university organizational authority, for example, it may safely be inferred the most appropriate model is the developmental one. However, if the test does produce a reduction in the regression coefficient, the problem of choosing between the spuriousness and hybrid models must be faced, for both predict a reduction. The problem is resolved by also testing for a developmental sequence by controlling for the attitudinal variable. Both the hybrid and developmental models predict a reduction in the regression coefficient of the background variable on the measures of support for dissent, while the spurious model predicts no reduction. Only when a reduction in the regression coefficients is observed under both tests should the hybrid model be inferred.

Confidence limits are utilized to test reduction of coefficients. Within the confidence limits the magnitudes of the coefficients could vary on a chance basis. The process is not just whether the controls reduce the magnitude of the regression coefficients, but whether they reduce them by an amount greater than they could have by chance given a significance level of .05. If the partial regression coefficient is smaller than the limit, we conclude that the relationship is unaffected by the control variable. Table 19 shows the possible results of the tests and the inference to be made.

In testing the models, the background characteristics will consist of the six previously delineated variables: obedience, father's education, mother's education, income, major, and G.P.A. A second test will be made utilizing the additional background characteristics of age, sex, religious identification, and party identification. Even though few zero-order correlations with the other variables in the first group proved to be significant, it may be instructive to observe those that were significant as well as the direction of change of those that were not. The additional background characteristics will give a broader basis for inference. The attitudinal variables will include the three most significant in predicting support for protest, namely, attitude toward university authority, radical regime change attitude, and ideological attitude. The behavioral variables will include the

TABLE 19
**Behavior of Regression Coefficients Under Tests for Spuriousness
and Developmental Sequence and Model to be Inferred**

Inference	Test for Spuriousness	Test for Developmental Sequence
Spuriousness	Reduction	No Reduction
Developmental	No Reduction	Reduction
Hybrid	Reduction	Reduction
Independence	No Reduction	No Reduction

three measures of support for actions of dissent: acceptance of others' participation, having participated oneself, and willingness to participate in the future.

The test for spuriousness between the three attitudinal variables and each of the three measures of support for actions of dissent controlling for the six original background factors appears in Tables 20, 21, and 22. For the lower confidence limits the figures in parentheses indicate that the regression coefficient must be reduced to zero by the control variables. Those confidence limits labeled NS indicate that the standard error of the regression coefficient was larger than the regression coefficient itself, thus including zero. The coefficient may not be considered reliable.

Table 20 shows the relationship between attitudes toward university organizational authority and support for actions of dissent controlling for the six background characteristics. For each of the measures of support for actions of dissent, none of the six background characteristics significantly reduces the regression coefficient between attitude toward university authority and the measures. Instead, the reductions are either very slight or nonexistent. This is true for both the total sample and the individual campus samples. The result is the same for the relationship between radical regime change attitude and support for actions of dissent as shown in Table 21. For both total and campus samples the reductions are slight or nonexistent. Finally, in examining the relationship between liberalism-conservatism and measures of support for dissent actions controlling for the background characteristics as shown in Table 22, again no significant

TABLE 20
Regression Coefficients Between Attitudes Toward University Authorities and Support for Actions of Dissent with Controls for 6 Background Factors

| | Simple b | Lower Confidence Limit | Regression Coefficients — Partial | | | | | |
			Obedience	Father's Education	Mother's Education	Income	Major	G.P.A.
Total Sample								
Acceptance	.149	.072	.140	.145	.150	.149	.146	.149
Have Participated	.244	.163	.234	.239	.246	.241	.244	.244
Would Participate	.280	.163	.260	.273	.283	.276	.277	.280
Campus I Sample								
Acceptance	.312	.100	.309	.317	.312	.335	.312	.308
Have Participated	.416	.142	.417	.412	.410	.419	.416	.414
Would Participate	.484	.114	.480	.482	.493	.507	.484	.476
Campus II Sample								
Acceptance	.048	NS	.026	.039	.046	.049	.046	.047
Have Participated	.160	.034	.152	.154	.155	.160	.161	.160
Would Participate	.216	.036	.193	.204	.212	.217	.213	.216
Campus III Sample								
Acceptance	-.004	NS	-.006	-.004	-.002	-.001	-.014	-.005
Have Participated	.144	(-.021)	.144	.147	.147	.142	.143	.144
Would Participate	.153	(-.119)	.148	.155	.156	.151	.146	.151
Campus IV Sample								
Acceptance	.257	.064	.256	.259	.265	.274	.257	.257
Have Participated	.237	.034	.221	.240	.259	.239	.241	.237
Would Participate	.269	(-.022)	.245	.269	.269	.273	.267	.269
Campus V Sample								
Acceptance	.124	(-.079)	.117	.127	.122	.124	.143	.120
Have Participated	.222	.009	.210	.223	.222	.224	.224	.225
Would Participate	.193	(-.113)	.169	.205	.185	.199	.220	.195

TABLE 21
Regression Coefficients Between Attitudes Toward Radical Regime Change and Support for Actions of Dissent with Controls for 6 Background Factors

| | Simple b | Lower Confidence Limit | Regression Coefficients — Partial | | | | | |
			Obedience	Father's Education	Mother's Education	Income	Major	G.P.A.
Total Sample								
Acceptance	.402	.330	.394	.397	.399	.402	.397	.406
Have Participated	.326	.246	.317	.319	.321	.328	.326	.335
Would Participate	.605	.495	.588	.597	.600	.607	.600	.618
Campus I Sample								
Acceptance	.475	.266	.481	.475	.473	.473	.471	.476
Have Participated	.562	.283	.562	.562	.556	.563	.555	.562
Would Participate	.697	.321	.707	.697	.700	.696	.698	.698
Campus II Sample								
Acceptance	.404	.276	.376	.396	.404	.401	.405	.414
Have Participated	.285	.145	.277	.279	.279	.284	.294	.286
Would Participate	.661	.472	.636	.649	.658	.658	.658	.670
Campus III Sample								
Acceptance	.280	.118	.280	.280	.280	.277	.275	.275
Have Participated	.102	(-.053)	.102	.106	.102	.104	.101	.109
Would Participate	.438	.195	.438	.442	.438	.440	.435	.441
Campus IV Sample								
Acceptance	.318	.148	.318	.326	.321	.312	.318	.321
Have Participated	.275	.095	.270	.288	.284	.275	.276	.283
Would Participate	.584	.337	.576	.590	.584	.584	.583	.603
Campus V Sample								
Acceptance	.432	.258	.432	.430	.435	.441	.425	.427
Have Participated	.310	.118	.302	.315	.318	.327	.311	.316
Would Participate	.508	.237	.494	.478	.471	.545	.498	.513

TABLE 22

Regression Coefficients Between Attitudes Toward Conservatism-Liberalism and Support for Actions of Dissent with Controls for 6 Background Factors

	Simple b	Lower Confidence Limit	Obedience	Father's Education	Mother's Education	Income	Major	G.P.A.
					Partial			
Total Sample								
Acceptance	.797	.649	.780	.794	.791	.797	.787	.797
Have Participated	.730	.567	.709	.725	.720	.732	.729	.733
Would Participate	1.338	1.117	1.299	1.338	1.328	1.342	1.329	1.342
Campus I Sample								
Acceptance	1.094	.613	1.089	1.095	1.090	1.088	1.083	1.094
Have Participated	1.179	.527	1.186	1.177	1.172	1.185	1.162	1.179
Would Participate	1.690	.835	1.680	1.688	1.690	1.687	1.696	1.689
Campus II Sample								
Acceptance	.678	.426	.638	.665	.678	.691	.676	.698
Have Participated	.703	.438	.690	.694	.689	.710	.705	.710
Would Participate	1.191	.821	1.149	1.172	1.186	1.207	1.186	1.214
Campus III Sample								
Acceptance	.706	.381	.712	.710	.707	.689	.703	.700
Have Participated	.197	(-.124)	.199	.214	.198	.213	.196	.197
Would Participate	1.045	.550	1.061	1.064	1.046	1.066	1.042	1.039
Campus IV Sample								
Acceptance	.631	.281	.649	.656	.642	.631	.634	.634
Have Participated	.785	.427	.704	.827	.815	.785	.796	.783
Would Participate	1.452	.966	1.346	1.478	1.459	1.452	1.459	1.443
Campus V Sample								
Acceptance	.884	.550	.881	.879	.880	.884	.858	.888
Have Participated	.719	.352	.706	.719	.719	.702	.726	.716
Would Participate	1.324	.820	1.303	1.306	1.299	1.283	1.290	1.322

reductions take place. This is generally what would be expected since there were few instances of significant correlation between the background characteristics and support for dissent. However, even in those instances where there were significant correlations no significant reduction takes place here between the attitudinal variables and support for actions of dissent. Therefore, the conclusion is the relationship between the attitudinal variables and support for actions of dissent is unaffected by the control variables.

As mentioned previously, the second set of background characteristics that will be utilized in these tests include age, sex, religious identification, and party identification. In the test for spuriousness, the hypothesis is that one or more of these variables is the real cause of the relationship and when they are controlled, the relationship between the attitudinal variables and support for actions of dissent is reduced. Thus, it might be anticipated that those who are younger, are male, are Catholics, or are Democrats would support actions of dissent regardless of attitudinal orientation toward authority or ideology.

The test for spuriousness between the three attitudinal variables and each of the three measures of support for actions of dissent controlling for the second set of background factors appear in Tables 23, 24, and 25.

TABLE 23
Regression Coefficients Between Attitudes Toward University Organizational Authorities and Support for Actions of Dissent with Controls for 4 Background Factors

			Regression Coefficients			
	Simple b	Lower Confidence Limit	Age	Sex	Religion	Party
Total Sample						
Acceptance	.149	.072	.144	.144	.128	.146
Have Participated	.244	.163	.239	.236	.220	.242
Would Participate	.280	.163	.273	.266	.244	.274
Campus I Sample						
Acceptance	.312	.100	.311	.311	.302	.318
Have Participated	.416	.142	.416	.417	.400	.404
Would Participate	.484	.114	.484	.486	.460	.461
Campus II Sample						
Acceptance	.047	NS	.045	.039	.026	.047
Have Participated	.160	.034	.157	.147	.141	.160
Would Participate	.216	.036	.211	.191	.179	.216
Campus III Sample						
Acceptance	-.004	NS	.001	-.020	-.046	-.005
Have Participated	.144	(-.021)	.149	.138	.124	.145
Would Participate	.153	(-.119)	.161	.137	.108	.152
Campus IV Sample						
Acceptance	.257	.064	.249	.269	.248	.264
Have Participated	.238	.034	.231	.231	.223	.244
Would Participate	.269	(-.022)	.261	.269	.252	.283
Campus V Sample						
Acceptance	.124	(-.079)	.121	.118	.120	.109
Have Participated	.222	.009	.219	.207	.216	.218
Would Participate	.193	(-.113)	.118	.175	.185	.176

Table 23 shows the relationship for attitudes toward university organizational authorities. Although some reductions in the regression coefficients occur when the control variables are introduced, none of the reductions are statistically significant at the .05 level. This is true for both the total and individual campus samples. For the total sample and for most cases within the campus samples, religious identification results in the largest reductions, but these are not even close to what is needed for significance. The relationship between attitude toward university authority and support for measures of dissent is unaffected by these background variables.

Table 24 shows the relationship for radical regime change attitudes. Again, while there are some reductions shown in the coefficients, none reach statistical significance. In this instance, religion and age seem to result in the most substantial reductions, although none are significant at the .05 level.

Finally, the relationship for liberalism-conservatism is shown in Table 25. As with the other two attitudinal variables, the relationship between liberalism-conservatism and measures of support for actions of dissent is

TABLE 24

Regression Coefficients Between Attitudes Toward Radical Regime Change and Support for Actions of Dissent with Controls for 4 Background Factors

	Simple b	Lower Confidence Limit	Regression Coefficients			
			Age	Sex	Religion	Party
Total Sample						
Acceptance	.402	.330	.368	.399	.369	.382
Have Participated	.326	.246	.280	.321	.282	.318
Would Participate	.605	.495	.552	.598	.543	.559
Campus I Sample						
Acceptance	.475	.266	.475	.475	.452	.494
Have Participated	.562	.283	.562	.560	.518	.547
Would Participate	.697	.321	.697	.696	.623	.663
Campus II Sample						
Acceptance	.404	.276	.373	.401	.379	.380
Have Participated	.285	.145	.213	.280	.259	.257
Would Participate	.666	.472	.576	.652	.614	.593
Campus III Sample						
Acceptance	.280	.118	.264	.254	.249	.266
Have Participated	.102	(-.053)	.075	.090	.079	.129
Would Participate	.438	.195	.412	.415	.406	.438
Campus IV Sample						
Acceptance	.318	.148	.265	.320	.274	.291
Have Participated	.275	.095	.238	.274	.194	.248
Would Participate	.584	.337	.545	.583	.507	.523
Campus V Sample						
Acceptance	.432	.258	.403	.433	.400	.412
Have Participated	.310	.118	.275	.312	.252	.305
Would Participate	.508	.237	.437	.510	.436	.485

TABLE 25

Regression Coefficients Between Conservatism-Liberalism and Support for Actions of Dissent with Controls for 4 Background Factors

	Simple b	Lower Confidence Limit	Regression Coefficients			
			Age	Sex	Religion	Party
Total Sample						
Acceptance	.797	.649	.735	.794	.730	.780
Have Participated	.730	.567	.654	.725	.643	.760
Would Participate	1.338	1.117	1.246	1.331	1.219	1.268
Campus I Sample						
Acceptance	1.094	.613	1.099	1.097	1.047	1.231
Have Participated	1.179	.527	1.183	1.190	1.094	1.159
Would Participate	1.690	.835	1.701	1.703	1.557	1.614
Campus II Sample						
Acceptance	.678	.426	.611	.672	.621	.621
Have Participated	.703	.438	.590	.694	.651	.682
Would Participate	1.191	.821	1.032	1.174	1.085	1.049
Campus III Sample						
Acceptance	.706	.381	.695	.690	.678	.720
Have Participated	.197	(-.124)	.184	.189	.178	.299
Would Participate	1.045	.550	1.025	1.028	1.012	1.118
Campus IV Sample						
Acceptance	.631	.281	.534	.629	.547	.485
Have Participated	.785	.427	.727	.790	.649	.694
Would Participate	1.452	.966	1.389	1.456	1.321	1.168
Campus V Sample						
Acceptance	.884	.550	.828	.879	.801	.819
Have Participated	.719	.352	.651	.701	.524	.761
Would Participate	1.324	.820	1.193	1.304	1.114	1.293

not significantly affected by these control variables. There are reductions for both the total and campus samples, but again none are statistically significant. For ideological attitudes, religion, age, and party provide some reductions in one case or another, but do not approach statistical significance.

It must be concluded, then, that the relationship between the three attitudinal variables and the measures of support for actions of dissent are generally not affected by the background characteristics tested.

At this point the tests for a developmental sequence will be taken up. Here the attitudinal variables will be controlled in testing the relationship between the background characteristics and the measures of support for actions of dissent.

Table 26 shows the tests for a developmental sequence for the first six background characteristics for the total sample. There are reductions in the total sample coefficients and also the within campus coefficients (which are not shown), for those instances where the zero-order coefficients were significant but none are sufficient to reach significance at the .05 level. This should not be too surprising in that little relationship was found between the two sets of variables during the formal testing of hypotheses. However, even for those coefficients that were significant, no statistically significant reduction takes place as a result of the introduction of the attitudinal controls.

Since previously the background variables caused no reduction in the coefficients of the relationship between the attitudinal variables and the measures of support for actions of dissent, the independence model would be the appropriate explanatory model.

Table 27 shows the tests for a developmental sequence for the second set of background characteristics for the total sample. Statistically significant reductions are observed for the introduction of radical regime change with age, religion, and party on acceptance, and on age and party on willingness. In addition, significant reductions are observed for the introduction of liberalism-conservatism with parth on acceptance, having participated, and willingness to participate. For the campus samples, which are not shown at Campus II, radical regime change with party on acceptance and willingness, and liberalism-conservatism with party on having participated and willingness to participate were significant. At Campus IV only liberalism-conservatism with party on willingness to participate was significant.

Previously no reductions were found between the attitudinal characteristics and the behavioral variables controlling for these background characteristics. In these few instances then a developmental sequence could be said to exist. However, when taken within the context of the lack of significant reductions for the majority of cases, the independence model would again seem to be the appropriate explanatory model.

TABLE 26

Regression Coefficients Between Six Background Factors and Support for Actions of
Dissent with Controls for Three Attitudinal Factors—Total Sample

		Regression Coefficients			
	Simple b	Lower Confidence Limit	Rad. Reg. Chg. Partial b	Univ. Auth. Partial b	Con-lib. Partial b
Acceptance:					
Obedience	.139	.046	.098	.123	.088
Father's Education	.070	.015	.054	.066	.066
Mother's Education	.070	.003	.053	.072	.055
Income	.002	NS	.008	-.005	.006
Major	.068	.012	.045	.064	.048
G.P.A.	-.006	NS	.040	-.008	.006
Have Participated					
Obedience	.157	.057	.124	.131	.110
Father's Education	.101	.042	.088	.094	.097
Mother's Education	.107	.036	.094	.110	.094
Income	.070	.000	.075	.060	.074
Major	.023	NS	.004	.016	.005
G.P.A.	.039	NS	.077	.036	.051
Would Participate					
Obedience	.296	.155	.235	.267	.211
Father's Education	.126	.042	.101	.117	.118
Mother's Education	.125	.024	.101	.129	.101
Income	.091	(-.008)	.099	.079	.099
Major	.083	(-.057)	.048	.076	.050
G.P.A.	.048	NS	.119	.045	.070

TABLE 27

Regression Coefficients Between Four Background Factors and Support for Actions of Dissent with Controls for Three Attitudinal Factors—Total Sample

	Simple b	Lower Confidence Limit	Rad. Reg. Chg. Partial b	Univ. Auth. Partial b	Con-lib. Partial b
			Regression Coefficients		
Acceptance					
Age	-.115	-.076	-.067*	-.114	-.078
Sex	-.146	(.009)	-.111	-.123	-.130
Religion	.154	.105	.105*	.146	.107
Party	.315	.174	.157*	.309	.039*
Have Participated					
Age	-.129	-.087	-.092	-.126	-.096
Sex	-.250	-.084	-.222	-.212	-.235
Religion	.180	.127	.142	.167	.139
Party	.198	.045	.067	.189	-.070*
Would Participate					
Age	-.179	-.120	-.106*	-.176	-.117*
Sex	-.380	-.144	-.327	-.336	-.352
Religion	.271	.195	.197	.256	.192*
Party	.608	.395	.338*	.598	.160*

INTERPRETATION OF RESULTS

The unrest on various college and university campuses has been attributed by various theorists and researchers as well as by the media to a variety of causes. Explanations ranging from the "generation gap" to a rise in permissiveness in the society have been mounted by the media to explain attitudes of an alienated youth portrayed as rising up in revolt. On the other hand, one line of research which was reviewed earlier tended to center on family socialization experiences and university educational experiences to explain alienated attitudes and protest actions. Researchers supporting these explanations tended to interview groups of activists rather than samples of students.

The results here do not tend to confirm the results of these activist-based studies. Permissiveness on the part of parents as perceived by the student did not prove to influence much either the student's willingness to reject the legitimacy of authorities of the political system whether on the national, state, city, or university levels or willingness to support the political system itself. Nor did permissiveness tend to influence much the student's support for stronger methods of dissent such as protesting, sitting-in, or civil disobedience. Likewise the other components of the student's family socialization experience, whether the education of his parents or his family income, also showed little influence on either attitudes toward authority or support for actions of dissent.

In addition, these results do not confirm some reported previous findings that the protest group constitutes an educational elite. Neither major in college nor grade point average produces a significant effect on the acceptance of the legitimacy of the authority of authorities of the political system on support for the regime of the political system, nor do they influence actual protest activity.

However, the positive results found for attitudes toward the legitimacy of university authorities, toward the regime, and toward ideology correlated with support for protest actions independent of family or educational background indicate that the crucial variables in explaining protest activity are attitudinal ones to be found in the minds of students and not matters of social class or educational background. Attitudinal variables concerned with political objects rather than social variables were more relevant for behavior.

In short, it is how the client feels about those who govern in the university organization, how he feels about the legitimacy of the political system as a whole, and how he feels in ideological terms that is crucial in his decision to engage in noncompliance activities, not social background variables removed from the political arena.

5. CONCLUSIONS

The first question addressed was the structure of client beliefs toward authority, that is, do they see organizational and other political system authorities in the same way or not. It was found that these clients did not view individual position authority purely according to function or according to level in the political system, but according to general, bureaucratic, organizational, police, and city authority dimensions. However, university organizational authority was found to have loadings on both general and organizational authority factors indicating these clients see them as both part of a particular subsystem, the organization of which they are a part, and the wider political system. Organizational authorities then will not necessarily be viewed on their own by clientele, but will also be viewed as representatives of the wider political system.

It was further found that clients attribute legitimacy differentially to various authorities. That is, some authorities enjoy a high degree of legitimacy while others enjoy a much lower degree. This finding has import for the degree of difficulty or cost such authorities will incur in organizational decision-making in reference to clients.

To examine possible causes of authority orientations, several socialization variables were examined. These stem from a line of socialization research which suggested that basic authority attitudes determined by early family treatment structure both organizational and political authority attitudes. The indictment of the American upper-middle-class family has been quite severe. Children socialized toward authority by permissive, highly educated parents in affluent homes are said to carry over their general rejection of authority to the organization and the political system, where it is manifested in overt noncompliance in terms of protest activity. However, granting that the parents and the home are important for the initial authority inception period, does it follow that these experiences are carried directly into organizational behavior? This thesis posits that family acts as the prototypical authority structure.

The data presented here do not tend to support such a thesis. Background factors such as perceived parental permissiveness, parents education, or university major were not explanatory of authority, or ideological attitudes, or dissent. This is not to say that socialization experiences play no role in determining such phenomena. An alternative possible route of development that is still family centered is that the parents transmit directly the content of their authority values rather than indirectly acting as authority prototypes. Jaros et al. (1968) found support for direct transmittal of parental political values but little for the family acting as a prototypical authority structure in a sample of Appalachian families. Tedin

(1974), looking at the influence of parents on party identification and public policy attitudes, found that the level of parental influence at any one point in time will be highly dependent on the distribution of issue salience and perceptual accuracy for the particular attitude object in question. On the basis of their national probability sample of 12+ grade students, Jennings and Niemi (1968: 179) concluded that it may be that the child acquires a minimal set of basic commitments to a way of handling authority situations as a result of early experiences in families, but that this is a foundation from which arises widely diverse value structures. Other explanations (Weissberg, 1972) center on those experiences the individual undergoes with respect to various authorities.

In predicting client noncompliance in terms of protest, authority and ideological attitudes are much more helpful than background factors. Ideological attitudes seemed to show particularly strong relationships followed by institutional regime attitudes, and then attitudes toward organizational authority. It thus appears that both diffuse and specific support orientations are involved in client compliance. However, in this case the specific support component seemed to be the stronger determinant. The significance of such a condition for the organization is that as the issues change which trigger these attitudes, noncomplaince behavior is likely to decrease. In fact, we know now that this is exactly what occurred following the winding down of Vietnam, elimination of the draft, and other issue changes.

Looking at the authority attitudes—regime authority and position authority—attitudes toward radical regime change were stronger determinants of noncompliance than were attitudes toward specific authorities. Attitudes toward organizational authorities did seem to be relevant to noncompliance. However, attitudes toward the regime of the political system were more significant. Events in the environment of the organization then will presumably be more controlling in terms of noncompliance orientations for this client group. That is, at least at this time, clients responded to the legitimacy of the authority of the political system as a whole and then to the legitimacy of organizational authorities. The ability of organizational authorities to influence compliance/noncompliance under conditions where issues in the wider environmental political system are stressful and the perceived legitimacy of that system is under substantial challenge is considerably constrained.

NOTE

1. In the factor analysis communalities are estimated from the squared multiple correlation coefficients. The minimum eigenvalue for which a factor was rotated was 1.0. The computer program used to perform the factor analysis and compute the factor scores is in the U.C.L.A. Bio-Medical (BMD series-BMD03M).

REFERENCES

ADORNO, T. W., E. FRENKEL-BRUNSWIK, D. J. LEVINSON, and R. N. SANFORD (1950) The Authoritarian Personality. New York: Norton.

ARMSTRONG, J. S. (1967) "Derivation of theory by means of factor analysis, or Tom Swift and his electric factor analysis machine." American Statistician 21: 17-21.

AXELROD, R. (1967) "The structure of public opinion on policy issues." Public Opinion Q. 31 (Spring): 51-60.

BAY, C. (1958) The Structure of Freedom. Stanford, Calif.: Stanford Univ. Press.

BERNARD, C. I. (1968) The Functions of the Executive. Cambridge: Harvard Univ. Press.

BLAU, P. and W. R. SCOTT (1962) Formal Organizations. San Francisco: Chandler.

BLOCK, J. H., N. HAAN, and M. B. SMITH (1968) "Activism and apathy in contemporary adolescents" in James F. Adams (ed.) Contributions to the Understanding of Adolescence. Boston: Allyn & Bacon.

BROWN, R. (1965) Social Psychology. New York: Free Press.

CHRISTIE, R., L. FRIEDMAN, and A. ROSS (1969) "The new left and its ideology." Scale reported in J. P. Robinson and P. R. Shaver, Measures of Social Psychological Attitudes. Ann Arbor: Inst. for Social Reasearch.

CHRISTIE, R., J. HAVEL and B. SEIDENBERG (1958) "Is the F Scale irreversible?" J. of Abnormal and Social Psychology 56: 143-159.

CHRISTIE, R and M. JAHODA [eds.] (1954) Studies in the Scope and Method of "The Authoritarian Personality." New York: Free Press.

CLARKE, J. W. and J. EGAN (1972) "Social and political dimensions of campus protest activity." J. of Politics (May): 500-523.

CNUDDE, C. F. and D. McCRONE (1969) "Party competition and welfare policies in the American states." Amer. Pol. Sci. Rev. 63: 858-866.

COOLEY, C. (1967) Human Nature and the Social Order. New York: Schocken.

CUNNINGHAM, J. V. (1972) "Citizen participation in public affairs." Public Admin. Rev. 32 (October): 589-602.

DAHL, R. (1963) Modern Political Analysis. Englewood Cliffs: Prentice-Hall.

DAY, J. (1963) "Authority." Political Studies 11: 257-271.

de JOUVENEL, B. (1957) Sovereignty. Chicago: Univ. of Chicago Press.

DUBIN, E. R. and R. DUBIN (1963) "The authority inception period in socialization." Child Development 34: 885-898.

DUNLAP, R. (1970) "Radical and conservative student activists: a comparison of family backgrounds." Pacific Soc. Rev. 13 (Summer): 171-181.

EASTON, D. (1956) A Framework for Political Analysis. Englewood Cliffs: Prentice-Hall.
––– (1957) "The function of formal education in a political system." School Review: 304-317.
EASTON, D. and J. DENNIS (1969) Children in the Political System. New York: McGraw-Hill.
––– (1962) "The child's political world." Midwest J. of Pol. Sci.: 229-246.
EPSTEIN, L. D. (1970) "The state university: who governs?" Paper delivered at sixty-sixty annual meeting of the Amer. Pol. Sci. Assn.
FIELD, J. and R. E. ANDERSON (1969) "Ideology in the public's conceptualization of the 1964 election." Public Opinion Q. 33 (Fall): 380-398.
FLACKS, R. (1967) "The liberated generation: an exploration of the roots of student protest." J. of Social Issues 23 (July): 52-75.
FREE, L. and H. CANTRIL (1968) The Political Beliefs of Americans. New York: Simon & Schuster.
FRIEDRICH, C. (1963) Man and His Government. New York: McGraw-Hill.
GREENSTEIN, F. (1965) Children and Politics. New Haven: Yale Univ. Press.
GURR, T. (1970) Why Men Rebel. Princeton: Princeton Univ. Press.
––– (1968) "A causal model of civil strife: a comparative analysis using new indices." Amer. Pol. Sci. Rev. 62: 1104-1124.
HALLECK, S. L. (1968) "Twelve hypotheses of student unrest" in G. K. Smith (ed.) Stress and Campus Response. San Francisco: Jossey-Bass.
HARRIS, L. (1971) "Political labels depend on who applies them." St. Petersburg Times (January 18): A10.
HEAD, T. B. et al. (1972) Justifying Violence: Attitudes of American Men. Ann Arbor: Univ. of Michigan Press.
HERBERT, A. (1972) "Management under conditions of decentralization and citizen participation." Public Admin. Rev. 32 (October): 622-637.
HERO, A. O. (1969) "Liberalism-conservatism revisited: foreign vs. domestic federal policies 1937-1967." Public Opinion Q. 33 (Fall): 399-408.
HESS, R. (1963) "The socialization of attitudes toward political authority: some cross-national comparisons." International Social Science J. 15: 542-559.
––– and J. TORNEY (1967) The Development of Political Attitudes in Children. Chicago: Aldine.
HYNEMAN, C. (1968) Popular Government in America. New York: Atherton.
JAROS, D., H. HIRSCH, and F. J. FLERON, Jr. (1968) "The malevolent leader: political socialization in an American subculture." Amer. Pol. Sci. Rev. 62: 564-575.
JENNINGS, M. K. and R. NIEMI (1968) "The transmission of political values from parent to child." Amer. Pol. Sci. Rev. 63: 169-184.
JOHNSON, R., F. E. KAST, and J. ROSENZWEIG (1973) The Theory and Management of Systems. New York: McGraw-Hill.
KATZ, E. and B. DANET (1973) Bureaucracy and the Public: A Reader in Official Client Relations. New York: Basic Books.
KENISTON, K. (1968) The Young Radicals. New York: Harcourt Brace.
LANGTON, K. P. (1969) Political Socialization. New York: Oxford Univ. Press.
MacIVER, R. (1947) The Web of Government. New York: Macmillan.
McCLOSKEY, H. (1969) Political Inquiry: The Nature and Uses of Survey Research. Toronto: Macmillan.
MEAD, G. H. (1967) Mind, Self and Society. Chicago: Univ. of Chicago Press.

PARSONS, T. (1958) "Authority, legitimation and political action" in C. Friedrich (ed.) Authority. Cambridge: Howard Univ. Press.

PERROW, C. (1972) Complex Organizations. Glenview: Scott, Foresman.

PETERSON, R. (1969) "The student protest movement: some facts, interpretations, and a plea." Paper presented at Amer. Psychological Assn. Convention, Washington, D.C. (August 31).

PIERCE, J. C. (1970) "Party identification and the changing role of ideology in American politics." Midweast J. of Pol. Sci. 14: 25-42.

PRESTHUS, R. (1960) "Authority in organizations." Public Admin. Rev. 20 (Spring): 86-91.

ROSE, R. (1969) "Dynamic tendencies in the authority of regimes." World Politics 21: 602-627.

SANFORD, N. (1973) "Authoritarian personality in contemporary perspective" in J. Knutson (ed.) Handbook of Political Psychology. San Francisco: Jossey-Bass.

SARTORI, G. (1965) Democratic Theory. New York: Praeger.

SEARING, D. D., J. J. SCHWARTZ, and A. E. LIND (1973) "The structuring principle: political socialization and belief systems." Amer. Pol. Sci. Rev. 67 (June): 415-432.

SHERIF, C. W., M. SHERIF, and R. NEBERGALL (1965) Attitude and Attitude Change: The Social Judgment-Involvement Approach. London: Saunders.

SHILS, E. A. (1954) "Authoritarianism: 'right' and 'left'" in R. Christie and M. Jahoda (eds.) Studies in the Scope and Method of "Authoritarian Personality." Glencoe: Free Press.

STRANGE, J. (1972) "Citizen participation in community action and model cities programs." Public Admin. Rev. 32 (October): 655-669.

TEDIN, K. L. (1974) "The influence of parents on the political attitudes of adolescents." Amer. Pol. Sci. Rev. 68 (December): 1579-1592.

THOMPSON, J. D. (1967) Organizations in Action. New York: McGraw-Hill.

TRENT, J. W. and J. L. CRAISE (1967) "Commitment and conformity in the American college." J. of Social Issues 23 (July): 34-51.

WATTS, W. A. and D. WHITTAKER (1966) "Some socio-psychological characteristics of members of the Berkeley Free Speech Movement and the student population at Berkeley." Applied Behavioral Science 2: 41-62.

WEBER, M. (1947) The Theory of Social and Economic Organization (translated by A. M. Henderson and T. Parsons). New York: Oxford Univ. Press.

WEISSBERG, R. (1972) "Adolescent experiences with political authorities." J. of Politics 34 (August): 797-824.

YATES, D. (1973) Neighborhood Democracy. Lexington: Lexington Books.

CHARLES WISE is an associate professor of public and environmental affairs at Indiana University. He has served as assistant to the president of Indiana University. He has served as a member of the National Council of the American Society for Public Administration.